Nathaniel Clark Burt

Hours among the Gospels

Or Wayside Truths from the Life of our Lord

Nathaniel Clark Burt

Hours among the Gospels
Or Wayside Truths from the Life of our Lord

ISBN/EAN: 9783337714680

Printed in Europe, USA, Canada, Australia, Japan

Cover: Foto ©ninafisch / pixelio.de

More available books at **www.hansebooks.com**

HOURS AMONG THE GOSPELS

OR

WAYSIDE TRUTHS

FROM THE

LIFE OF OUR LORD.

BY

N. C. BURT, D.D.

PHILADELPHIA
J. B. LIPPINCOTT & CO.
1866.

Entered according to the Act of Congress, in the year 1865, by

J. B. LIPPINCOTT & CO.,

In the Clerk's Office of the District Court for the Eastern District of Pennsylvania.

PREFACE.

Two musical notes produce a higher effect when sounding in harmony, than when heard singly in succession. Two slightly different views of the same scene, blended in the stereoscope, give a single view far more life-like than that which either presents when seen by itself.

Thus two separated portions of Divine truth are sometimes found to be so remarkably related to each other, that being brought together, a far more striking, if not a wholly new impression is obtained.

Such works as Paley's "*Horæ Paulinæ*" and Blunt's "Undesigned Coincidences of the Old and New Testaments," valuable as they are for the special object of establishing the minute truthfulness of the Sacred Writers, secure perhaps even a higher result, in incidentally eliciting the fuller and more vivid meanings of those portions of Scripture with which they deal.

In pursuing the study of the Gospel records, the author has, from time to time, noted such passages as have been found to receive striking illustration from unexpected sources. The chief of these, with their illustrations, are herewith presented. Sometimes, as will be seen, the illustration comes from outside the Gospel history. Often the narrative in one of the gospels finds its complement in the parallel narrative of another of the gospels. Occasionally the immediate context, when well considered, is found to have an interpretative bearing not at first sight perceived.

The passages illustrated being of considerable number, and coming from every part of the Evangelic narratives, and being moreover here arranged, as nearly as possible, in the order of historical occurrence, the book instead of proving to be a mere aggregation of disconnected teachings, may be found to present a tolerably complete outline of the Life and Ministry of our Lord.

It may not be amiss to state that the first chapter, substantially as here given, was published some years since, under the author's initials, in one of the religious magazines.

Although the Gospel records are receiving elaborate exposition and defence from the most distinguished Sons of the Church, it is hoped that this humble effort will not be regarded as either wholly useless or presumptuous.

CINCINNATI, *May*, 1865.

CONTENTS.

I.
The Visit of the Wise Men; as directly occasioned by Daniel's Prophecy of the Messiah.. 9

II.
The Baptism of Christ; as illustrated by His Transfiguration........... 16

III.
The Temptation in the Wilderness; as illustrated by Christ's Rebuke of Peter.. 21

IV.
The Contempt of Nathanael for Nazareth, connected with the fact that he belonged to Cana of Galilee.. 28

V.
The Healing of the Paralytic and of the Infirm Man Compared......... 32

VI.
The Woman who was a Sinner, and Christ's Gracious Invitation....... 37

VII.
Sudden Outbreak of Pharisaic Hostility; and its Immediate Occasion. 44

VIII.
Levi's Feast, in Several Relations; especially Christ's Representation of Himself as the Bridegroom.. 50

CONTENTS.

IX.

The Disciples unexpectedly Compelled to Embark and cross the Lake: and the Reason for it 58

X.

Crisis in the History of Judas 64

XI.

The Person who saw Men as Trees Walking not *born* blind 70

XII.

The Opening of a New Era in the Ministry of Christ 75

XIII.

The Transfiguration Occurring at Night 84

XIV.

The Transfiguration Scene Culminating in the Heavenly Voice 87

XV.

The Exclamation, "O Faithless and Perverse Generation;" as uttered soon after the Transfiguration 90

XVI.

The Contentions of the Disciples among themselves; as always connected with Christ's Teachings concerning His Death 94

XVII.

Conduct of the Unbelieving Brethren of Jesus; as seen on Two Occasions 100

XVIII.

The Allegory of the Good Shepherd; as connected with the Healing of the man born blind 106

XIX.

The Request, "Lord, suffer me first to go and bury my father;" by whom made, and why refused 110

CONTENTS. 7

XX.

Christ "Beholding" the Young Ruler; as illustrated by His "turning and looking on Peter." 116

XXI.

Parable of the Laborers in the Vineyard; as connected with Previous Teachings 122

XXII.

Christ's Triumphal Entry into Jerusalem: The Ass and Her Colt 128

XXIII.

The Miracle and the Parable of the Barren Fig-Tree 132

XXIV.

Christ's Denunciations against the Scribes and Pharisees at different times, compared 138

XXV.

The Anointing of Christ by Mary of Bethany: the Evangelists compared 145

XXVI.

The Resolution of Judas to Betray his Lord, and its Immediate Occasion 153

XXVII.

Christ's saying, "I am among you as he that Serveth," and His Washing the Disciples' Feet 160

XXVIII.

Position of Judas at the Passover Table 164

XXIX.

The Agony in the Garden; as illustrated by the Temptation in the Wilderness 172

XXX.

The Two Cries of the People, "Hosanna to the Son of David," and "Away with Him, Crucify Him."... 179

XXXI.

Judas Repenting at the Sight of Jesus Condemned........................ 185

XXXII.

Joseph of Arimathea, and His Mission.. 191

XXXIII.

Jesus, after his Resurrection, appearing first to Mary Magdalene...... 197

XXXIV.

Christ's saying to Mary Magdalene, "Touch me not: for I am not yet Ascended to my Father.".. 205

XXXV.

The Incredulity of Thomas; as Overcome in like manner with that of Nathanael.. 209

HOURS AMONG THE GOSPELS.

I.

The Visit of the Wise Men; as directly occasioned by Daniel's Prophecy of the Messiah.

Matt. ii. 1, 2; Daniel ix. 24–26.

IN the opening of the gospel history, we behold distinguished Gentile strangers arriving at Jerusalem, and uttering the remarkable inquiry, "Where is he that is born king of the Jews?" Who were these men? Whence came they? What did they mean by "king of the Jews?" And, above all, how had they become possessed of the knowledge that a king of the Jews was just now to be born, of such peculiar dignity as to demand their personal homage?*

---

* The opinion of scholars on this point is thus expressed by ELLICOTT: "It has long been a matter of discussion what precisely led these Magi to expect a birth so prefigured. See Spanheim, *Dub. Evang.* Was it due to a carefully preserved knowledge of the prophecy of Balaam, an opinion entertained by Origen and the majority of the ancient expositors; or was it due to prophecies uttered in their own country, dimly foreshadowing this divine mystery? (See citations from the Zend-Avesta.) Perhaps the latter view is the most probable, especially if we associate it with a belief, which the sacred narrative gives us every reason for entertaining, (Matt. ii. 12,) that these faithful men received a special illumination," &c. How has it come to pass that scholars have been so intent on the "dim foreshadowings" of the Zend-Avesta, as to overlook the explicit

This last question, as it seems to us, has not received sufficient comparative attention. Biblical scholars dwell chiefly on the character of the star which these strangers allege that they have seen; a matter of comparatively small importance.

In attempting to answer this question, reference is commonly made to that expectation of a mighty Deliverer soon to arise from among men, which, at the time of our Saviour's birth, as history attests, was widely indulged amongst the nations. If we ask how such an expectation came to exist, the reply is manifold. It may have arisen partly from the native conviction of the soul of its need of spiritual help—that which was desired to be, at length fixing itself as sure to be. It may have arisen partly from early tradition—the most important communications from God to the progenitors of the race having been promises of a Redeemer. And it may have arisen partly from the predictions of the Jewish Scriptures, which, for some hundreds of years, had been widely circulated among the learned of many lands.

This general expectation of a Redeemer, taken in connection with extraordinary appearances in the heavens, might, to some persons, seem sufficient to account for these wise men coming to Jerusalem with the inquiry which they proposed.

But we may look further than this. The narrative styles these persons "Wise men from the East." May we not obtain valuable hints from the very form of these predictions of the prophet Daniel, "uttered," as all the probabilities allege, in the very country of these Magi. Some indeed make a general reference to the book of Daniel, but none, so far as we have seen, trace the exact correspondence between the visit and question of the wise men and the terms of Daniel's prophecy.

expressions? The region designated as "the East," is of course very indefinite; but it at once occurs to us, that the East, as the birth-place of mankind, would furnish the purest and most vivid traditions of primitive times. It would be in the East, rather than the West, that the expectation of a Deliverer soon to be born, founded on ancient tradition, would be strongest; and men from the East, rather than from the West, might be looked for in Jerusalem, making the inquiry of these wise men.

There is, however, something noticeable in this very expression, "Wise men." It is the translation of the word "magoi." These Wise men were *Magians*. This appellation strongly points to *Persia*, as a narrower region of "the East" from which these strangers came.—Magian was the designation of the Persian priesthood and nobility.

Our attention being fixed on Persia, we at once recollect the fact that heathenism was there seen in its mildest and most spiritual forms. Also, from the bold and full tradition of the deluge which Persia furnishes, we infer the superiority of that country in all traditionary knowledge. These, then, were the very persons of all others to come to Jerusalem, making the inquiry which they made; for even if we were unable to see where they obtained such exact information as led them to *just* such a visit and *just* such an inquiry, we might well conclude, that possibly, in the most thoughtful of Persian minds, ancient traditions of a coming Deliverer may have ripened for fulfillment along with the prophecies of God's covenant people, until, the heavens giving birth to a new star, they were ready to interpret the occurrence as a token of the birth of the Expected One.

But we need not stop here. The question, how these heathen sages became possessed of such knowledge as led them to make a pilgrimage at this time to Jerusalem, and to propose the precise inquiry which they proposed, admits of an explicit and satisfactory answer. And the answer shows us how remarkably one portion of God's word confirms another, and how, by minute and unintended agreements, the whole Bible may be confirmed to us, as a book of perfect truth. Let us see.

We know that the Magians of Persia were learned men—that they were read in the accessible literature of all lands. We know that they were held in highest respect, as nobles of the State, and as counsellors and guardians of the king. This is the familiar teaching of history.

Bear this in mind, and then remember that the Jews were seventy years captives in Babylon, where they had their Scriptures, and that they were restored to their own country by Cyrus, the conqueror of Babylon and founder of the Persian Empire, who himself was familiar with the Jewish Scriptures. And remember, especially, that the prophet Daniel, who alone of all the prophets recorded the exact time of Messiah's advent, was himself a high civil officer under the first Persian monarchs in Babylon, and hence must have been widely and familiarly conversant with the Magians of his time.

Remembering all this, we may ask the following questions: If the Jewish Scriptures had such circulation in Babylon that Cyrus became acquainted with them, must we not suppose that the learned Magians, his counsellors and guardians, became even more thoroughly acquainted with them? And if the Magians studied the sacred books of the Jews generally, must we not think that their attention would be specially directed to the writings of *Daniel*, their cotemporary and companion, whose writings constituted a part of those sacred books? And, if the Magians of that day had special familiarity with the writings of Daniel, would not the Magians of a later day, their successors, have those particular expectations of the Coming One which the writings of Daniel would give?

All this probable conjecture receives confirmation from the fact that while Daniel alone, of all the prophets, records the exact time of Messiah's birth, he reckons the time from a date in the civil history of the Persians. It is " from the going forth of the commandment (of Cyrus) to restore and build Jerusalem," that the weeks of Daniel's prophecy proceed.

Now, examining that celebrated prophecy, we find an exact and literal correspondence between its principal terms and the several expressions of these wise men. And we find the prophecy to be of the precise character to set such men upon the making of precisely such a visit as Matthew represents these wise men actually making. The conclusion seems irresistible that the expectations and conduct and language of these men were founded directly upon that prophecy.

All that was needed, in their state of mind, to send them upon their visit, was the *suggestion of some visible sign*. They being astrologers, and ever watching the heavens for tokens of earthly occurrences, no wonder that when, at the exact time mentioned by Daniel as that of Messiah's birth, they saw an extraordinary appearance in the heavens, they cried, It is "*his star.*"* And when Daniel spoke of no other place than "the holy city," in connection with the Messiah, no wonder that they *came to Jerusalem* seeking him, and asking, "*Where is he?*" When Daniel called the predicted One the "Messiah," no wonder that they so explained themselves that Herod demanded of the assembled Council "where *Christ* should be born." And when Daniel spoke of Messiah as "the Prince," no wonder that they brought *royal* gifts, and asked, "Where is he that is born *king* of the Jews?"

These wise men, as just observed, were astrologers. They might also be called astronomers. In their studies, doubtless, science and superstition mingled. Chaldean Shepherds made the first recorded astronomical observations. And judicial astrology took its rise in the region from which these Magians came. The very word *magic*, looking so strongly to the frauds of superstition, has the

* The Commentators, with great unanimity, connect the star of the wise men with that predicted by Balaam. Num. xxiv. 17. The nature of any legitimate connection it is difficult to discern.

Supposing Balaam's prophecy to relate to the Messiah, are we to think that Christ came as a star, only in the way of an extraordinary celestial phenomenon, to be appreciated by a few heathen astrologers? Messianic prophecies are the perpetual heritage of the whole church. The Jews no doubt construed this prophecy *figuratively:* they had no thought, in connection with it, of any *literal* star. And the views of the wise men concerning this prophecy, had they any knowledge of it, beyond question would be adopted from the Jews.

But where is the evidence that the Jews regarded this as a Messianic prophecy? And why are *we* to give it a Messianic character? (See Hengstenberg's Christology.)

In any case, there seems to be no other connection between the star of the wise men and that of Balaam's prophecy than a chance verbal coincidence.

same origin as the word Magian. Yet we find that God gave these Magians a sign such as they would not fail to observe and improve—a sign in the heavens—a star. Behold here an evidence of God's condescending goodness. He meets men wherever they go. He suffers them to look nowhere for himself in vain.*

Yet it may be asked, Supposing that this sign in the heavens fell in with the superstitions of astrology, and wedded itself to them, would it not seem that God had here granted his sanction to error?† The words of NEANDER are apt and unanswerable. "If it offends us to find that God has used the errors of man to lead him to a knowledge of the great truths of salvation, as if thereby he had lent himself to sustain the false, then must we break in pieces the chain of human events, in which the true and the false, the good and the evil, are so inseparably linked that the latter often serves for the point of transition to the former. . . . God condescends to the platforms of men, in training them for belief in the Redeemer, and meets the aspirations of the truth-seeking soul, even in its error."

* The Magi are led by a star; the fishermen by fishes, to the knowledge of Christ. BENGEL. † STRAUSS.

II.

The Baptism of Christ; as illustrated by His Transfiguration.

Matt. iii. 13-17; Matt. xvii. 1-5; with their parallels.

THE Baptism and the Transfiguration have one grand feature in common. It is the solemn recognition from heaven, by God the Father, of Jesus as His approved Son.

A further, although less obvious correspondence between these striking occurrences, is seen in the relations which they respectively sustain to the public ministry of Christ. The Baptism stands at the entrance of that ministry considered as a whole. In it the Father, seemingly for the encouragement of the Son in all his appointed work, acknowledges and approves him. So the Transfiguration stands at the entrance of that marked period immediately preceding the death of Christ, for which all that had as yet occurred was mainly a preparation; the period in which the special sufferings of our Lord were held in direct prospect, were spoken of to the disciples, and presently, in all their bitterness, were endured. As the Baptism stands at the entrance of our Lord's ministry considered as a whole, so the Transfiguration stands at the entrance of what may be called his *passive* ministry. As, in the former, the Father gives in advance a token of approbation to his Son, adapted to encourage him in the whole work before him; so, in the latter, when the

Saviour's ministry is about to become most trying, and when his appointed sufferings might seem to betoken the Father's displeasure, he receives repeated and emphatic assurance of the Father's steadfast favor.

Not, however, to dwell on this, we desire especially to call attention to the difference in the heavenly testimony given on these two occasions, and to what this difference intimates. This difference is often overlooked; and the failure to observe it has helped to form what must be considered a very erroneous conception concerning the Baptism.

Comparing the narratives of these events, we shall see that while, in connection with the Transfiguration, each of the three writers recording the event is careful to give, as a part of the solemn utterance from heaven, the injunction, "hear ye him," these writers uniformly omit any such injunction in their accounts of the Baptism. At the Baptism, the heavenly testimony, according to Matthew, was in these words, "This is my beloved Son, in whom I am well pleased." At the Transfiguration, according to the same Evangelist, the voice out of the cloud uttered precisely the same words, with the addition "hear ye him."

It is thus seen that, at the Transfiguration, the heavenly voice was directed in part to the spectators of the scene— to Peter, James and John. And we know, from the Scriptures elsewhere, that these spectators understood the divine declaration.* At the Baptism, the spectators, whoever they may have been, were not addressed at all.

From this difference, it is not difficult to infer, either, that the Baptism was not witnessed by the multitudes

* 2 Pet. i. 16–18.

who were attending John's ministry, or, that witnessing it, they were not permitted to hear intelligibly the heavenly voice. And this inference we cannot but regard as correct.

The impression so common with casual readers of the history, and even with popular commentators, that the sublime attestation of the Messiahship of Jesus given in connection with his Baptism, was directed to the people at large, and was understood by them, is scarcely credible.* Had this been the case, would not the effect of it have been stated? No doubt had the people, eager for the coming of their Messiah, been thus publicly assured from the skies that their Messiah had come, and had they beheld Jesus designated as such by heavenly tokens, they would have become frantic with excitement, and at once enthroned Jesus as the Successor of David.† And how easy, in after years, had this occurrence been of the sort imagined, for Jesus to have referred his enemies to it, when they so persistently demanded of him a sign from heaven. Yet the event passed by, apparently without effect upon the people, and is never referred to again, except by the Baptist, who avers that, in his official character, he was permitted to witness the descent upon Jesus of the Holy Spirit.‡

The narrative speaks of the heavens being opened "*to him*"—to Jesus; as if the heavenly witness was given mainly for his sake. In the particular mention of the Baptist, as also enjoying the sight of the descending Spirit, is it not strongly intimated that the privilege was limited to the Saviour and his Forerunner?

Some persons may imagine, that since the people seem

---

* See BARNES, JACOBUS, and others. † John vi. 15. ‡ i. 32–34.

to have been present at the baptism of Jesus, they *must* have seen what is spoken of as visible, and heard what is spoken of as audible. But, even supposing that the multitudes were present, which is not declared, and is not at all certain,* it is enough to reply that here was a *miracle*, and it is impossible for us to say where the miracle might begin and where end, whether it might not extend to the eyes and ears of the people. When Paul was converted, he heard an articulate voice addressing him. His companions perceived only a sound or noise.† When the voice came to Jesus out of the skies, declaring, "I have both glorified it, and will glorify it again," those that stood by thought that it thundered.‡ So here; whatever the people may have seen or heard probably had for them no significance. For them, if anything at all, it was simply a blinding flash, as of lightning, and a stunning noise, as of thunder.

This point is of importance, from its relation to our Saviour's whole course of procedure, in his public ministry, in communicating the truth that he was the Messiah. It is remarkable that he never made to the people an explicit announcement of this truth. Farthest from it. Here and there, privately, and to those prepared to receive it, he made the truth known,§ but in his public relations he handled it with extreme caution. He permitted it to come upon the minds of the people only in an indirect way and in the most gradual manner, like the slow dawning of a great light. He often charged those who witnessed his most striking miracles, not to

---

* THOLUCK on John v. 36–38.　　† Acts ix. 7; xxii. 9.　　‡ John xii. 29.
§ John i. 41, 49; iv. 26.

let them be known.* He would not suffer the devils to speak, because they knew that he was the Christ.†

Now this whole procedure was self-consistent and is perfectly intelligible, apart from the common conception of the event before us; yet it becomes utterly inexplicable, if we suppose that, in the very beginning of his ministry, the truth of his Divine Sonship and Messiahship was flashed on the minds of the whole nation. Nothing but explicit statements of Scripture could justify this view. Not only are such statements wanting, but the view has no evidence of correctness whatever.

* Matt. viii. 4; Mark v. 43; Luke ix. 21. † Mark i. 25, 34.

III.

The Temptation in the Wilderness; as illustrated by Christ's Rebuke of Peter.

Matt. iv. 10; xvi. 23. Also their parallels.

On two occasions, widely separated, we find our Saviour uttering the self-same words of stern reprimand, "Get thee behind me, Satan."* The one of these was that of the Temptation in the Wilderness. On this occasion, three distinct assaults upon the Saviour were made by the great Adversary. The last of these, it would seem, was that in which the Tempter, having taken the Saviour up into a high mountain, showed him all the kingdoms of the world and the glory of them, and tendered these to him on condition that he would fall down and worship him. This assault appears to have been the most determined and desperate on the part of the Tempter, and the most trying and grievous to the Saviour. Whatever disguise the Adversary may have assumed, he was now fully recognized in his proper character, as the hideous Prince of wickedness, and speedily does the vehement rebuke of the Holy One put him to flight.†

* The self-same in the latest Greek editions.

† We have given above our own impression concerning the actual order of the second and third assaults of Satan, following Matthew's arrangement rather than that of Luke. The remarks on this point of Westcott, "Introduction to the Study of the Gospels," pp. 316, 317, are highly sug-

The other occasion of our Saviour's uttering the same reprimand, was not one in which the devil appeared in person. Only the disciples were present. And the reprimand was directed to a prominent apostle, who had just before witnessed that good confession of Jesus as the Christ which brought from the Master's lips the emphatic commendation, "Blessed art thou, Simon Bar-jona." Yet the reprimand, while directed to Peter, was administered again upon the great Adversary. Peter is not named, nor recognized, in the language of the Saviour. As though the disciple were absent, and only his old enemy again confronted him, Christ once more exclaims, "Get thee behind me, Satan!"

This extraordinary language, never used at any other time, indicates an essential identity in the occasions which called for it. If, in the wilderness, Jesus was *tempted* of the devil, so was he when "Peter took him, and began to rebuke him, saying, Be it far from thee, Lord: this shall not be unto thee." And whatever the *character* of the temptation in the wilderness, when the devil tendered the Saviour the kingdoms of the world and their glory, the *same* temptation was again urged, in the remonstrance and pleading of Peter. Such, at least, is the probable inference.

This being the case, the one of these occasions may be

gestive. "The representative points of the temptation, for the narratives imply much which they do not contain, are given in each case in the order which preserves a climax from the particular position occupied by the writer. . . . The sequence is one of idea, and not of time. The incidents are given wholly without any temporal connection in St. Luke, and the language of St. Matthew is more definite only in appearance. The narrative, indeed, is one which may perhaps help to show the impossibility of applying to things spiritual and eternal that 'phantom of succession,' in the shadow of which we are commonly forced to speak and act."

taken to illustrate the other; the clearer character of the temptation in the case of Peter, may be permitted to throw light on the character, and hence on the circumstances, of the temptation as it occurred in the wilderness.

We need not now trouble ourselves with the view of some expositors, that the whole scene of temptation in the wilderness was without objective reality, having occurred to our Saviour when he was in an extasy or trance, and that it possesses only a symbolic significance. The evidences of the *reality* of the occurrence are numerous and overwhelming. But rejecting this view, the question still remains, how far the records concerning this occurrence are to be *literally* interpreted. Did the Wicked One approach the Saviour in visible form, and utter in his ears an audible voice, and convey him through the air to a pinnacle of the temple, and take him again to the summit of a mountain and expose to his actual view the empires of the whole world? Or did the temptation begin and end in the desert, the Wicked One being personally, though not visibly, present; and exerting his full power upon the Saviour, yet not by audible words and visible scenes, but by the forcible *suggestion* of such thoughts and such objects as he hoped would be enticing?

Upon these questions, the temptation by Peter may throw needed light. If we adopt the *literal* view, we must believe, for example, concerning the third temptation in the wilderness, that the devil, having actually rapt the Saviour away from the pinnacle of the temple, carried him to the top of a mountain from which a view was had of the whole world. Here we encounter the difficulty, that a view of the whole world from the loftiest mountain-summit is a physical impossibility. Further, we must believe that the Tempter sought to obtain from the Saviour, under the fascinations of visible earthly splendor, and in the prospect of attaining the highest worldly grandeur, an act of outward personal homage; for the language of the Tempter is, "All these things will I give thee, if thou wilt fall down and worship me." The idea that the homage asked for was of such sort seems puerile. It has been well said that "no extraordinary degree of piety would have been necessary to rebuke such a proposal as this."

Turning to the temptation which Peter occasioned the Master, we may learn that this third temptation in the wilderness was something different from what the literal theory supposes. It was essentially this:—a forcible suggestion to the mind of Jesus, that he should abandon his intention of establishing his Messianic kingdom in the world simply upon a spiritual basis—by means of wearisome instruction, and self-denying toils, and an ignominious death; and, instead of this, accept the powerful aid of the god of this world in establishing that kingdom as a universal empire on the basis of the kingdoms and the glory of the world.

Let us review the narrative which exhibits the conduct of Peter and the significance of his remonstrance with the Master. The record in Matthew is as follows: "From that time forth began Jesus to show unto his disciples, how that he must go unto Jerusalem, and suffer many things of the elders and chief priests, and scribes, and be killed, and be raised again the third day." Our Saviour was just entering upon a new era in his ministry, in which his special sufferings and coming death were held in prominent view.* To help prepare his disciples for receiving his instructions upon this subject, he had just brought from them the solemn avowal of their faith in him as the Messiah.† His first announcement of the great truth that the Messiah must suffer, made in the language just cited, startled the disciples. It was both surprising and distasteful. It produced, no doubt, a sudden and profound revulsion of feeling. "What! their Master taken from them: his enemies successful against him and triumphing in his death! And he consenting to it! It must not be." Such were their thoughts. And Peter, ever more forward than the rest, ventured to lead the Master aside, and not only to remonstrate against such teaching, but actually to reprove the Master and protest against his proposed course. That course, thought Peter, would be fatal to the prospects both of the Master and of his disciples. Instead of this, Jesus might better proceed at once to "restore again the kingdom to Israel."

And then it was that Jesus, discerning herein not merely the working of an unworthy feeling on the part of an imperfect disciple, but, further than this, the direct agency of the devil, who for the time was making use of the disciple as the vehicle for renewing his most mighty temptation, administers the stunning rebuke already cited. The prospect of his dying for the life of the world, of his ushering in his kingdom by the birth-pangs of his own humiliations even unto death—this was at the moment in the full view of the Saviour; and the contemplation of it was painful enough for his flesh without the super-

* See Chs. II. and XII.   † Matt. xvi. 16.

added and wicked suggestions of the Tempter, that he might forego this in behalf of an easier way, that he might meet the desires and expectations of his disciples and of the whole people in assuming the throne of David and setting up a grand temporal kingdom; so that with instant and vehement resentment, he stops the mouth of the disciple, and repels the Tempter.

Viewing the third assault of the Adversary in the wilderness in the light of this temptation by Peter, and learning thereby to interpret as figurative the language concerning a personal homage to Satan on bended knees, and concerning an actual sight of the empires of the world from a mountain-height; learning thereby to regard this third onset of the Tempter as a suggestion to the mind of Jesus that he should forego the career of humiliation opening before him, and secularize his kingdom; we can readily discern in the proceeding that which would have, even with the Holy One, the character and the force of a mighty temptation.*

In his forty days' seclusion in the desert, the Saviour had doubtless been meditating upon his great work, about to be undertaken, of inaugurating the kingdom of God. Probably this work had presented itself to his mind in its many discouraging aspects. He well knew the opposition he would encounter in preaching his self-

* "Looking at the matter, then, from all sides, we may sum up the meaning of the temptation of Jesus thus: In the decisive rejection of the false and the adoption of the true idea of the Messiah, in the refusal of a worldly kingdom and the choice of the kingdom of God, a triumph was gained over the power of evil generally, and this achievement not only evinced the capability of Jesus to found a Divine kingdom, but constituted him for all times the prototype of victory over every species of temptation."

ULLMANN's Sinlessness of Jesus.

denying doctrines. He well knew the disappointment he would occasion the people, who in their Messiah were anticipating a glorious temporal deliverer. And, beyond doubt, his natural feelings contemplated the prospect with a painful shrinking. This being so, the Adversary, in this third assault, having some understanding of the burden oppressing the mind of Jesus, seeks by skillful suggestion to divert him from his purpose. He endeavors to persuade him to meet the carnal expectation of the people by allying himself with worldly power. He pictures to the imagination of Jesus the glorious career which would at once open to him, consenting thus to modify his plans. And he pledges his own powerful influence for the exaltation of Jesus, as Prince of a universal world-dominion and Lord of all earthly grandeur. But for the Saviour to yield to this suggestion, and accept the aid of the god of this world, what were it but to become the vassal of the Wicked One? what were it but to do him worship? And the bold assault, in which the Tempter seems to have gathered and applied his whole force, is promptly and successfully repelled. Adapted to be powerful, the temptation exerts no power. Hurled with might, it but rebounds with the greater violence, and with the more complete destruction to itself, like shattered glass from marble floor.

The prompt and indignant rebuke of the Saviour sends the Adversary from his presence, doubtless in mortification and rage.

IV.

The Contempt of Nathanael for Nazareth, connected with the fact that he belonged to Cana of Galilee.

John i. 46; xxi. 2.

WHEN Philip, full of joy at his recent acquaintance with Jesus, makes the announcement to Nathanael, "We have found him of whom Moses in the law and the prophets did write, Jesus of Nazareth, the son of Joseph," Nathanael exclaims, "Can there any good thing come out of Nazareth?"

The question occurs, why this extreme disparagement of the village to which our Saviour belonged, by this particular person?

It is commonly imagined that Nathanael herein merely exhibits an acquiescence in the general opinion that "no prophet," much less "The Prophet," should arise out of Galilee, Nazareth being a village of Galilee.* It may well be doubted, however, whether at this time there was any such prevalent opinion. Probably this opinion was not advanced until Jesus had fully entered on his public ministry and the impression was becoming current that he was a mighty prophet of God. And it seems altogether natural to suppose that it was then announced as a *dictum* of the Scribes, and that its promulgation was one of the measures concerted by the enemies of Jesus

* John vii. 52.

for discrediting his divine commission and checking his growing popularity.* Besides, the language of Nathanael expresses more than a mere incredulity concerning Galilee being the native country of any prophet. His language is that not of incredulity, but of positive contempt. It instances not Galilee but Nazareth. It doubts whether *any* good thing by possibility can come out of Nazareth. And that this contempt was felt for Nazareth rather than Galilee, seems further probable from the fact that Nathanael belonged to Galilee. As ALFORD observes, "It is impossible that Nathanael, himself a Galilean, could speak from any feeling of contempt for Galilee generally." And although the word "Nazarene" was by and by used contemptuously, in connection with the name of our Saviour, even according to the predictions referred to by Matthew,† Nazareth being a mere village of outlying Galilee, and being viewed in contrast with the historic towns of Judea, and especially in contrast with Jerusalem, there seems to be no good evidence that among Galileans generally Nazareth was held in special dishonor. None of the other apostles are at any time represented as asking any such question as this of Nathanael.

How then came it to pass that just Nathanael, and nobody else, should have been prompted to ask this question?

The inquiry is of no great importance, except as its answer may bring to view another of those unintended and minute evidences of truthfulness, which abound in these records. In this instance, a most natural and graphic touch is imparted to the historic picture, exhibiting

* John vii. 40–43. † Matt. ii. 23.

what is universally recognized as the truth of common life.

When we reflect for a moment, do we not see that the question of Nathanael would come most naturally from one who was familiarly acquainted with the localities about Nazareth? Who else would be likely to interest himself in the comparative merits of Nazareth and other villages of Galilee? And do we not see further, that if Nazareth would be despised by any, it would be by the inhabitants of neighboring and rival villages? A citizen of Capernaum might speak disparagingly of the villages of Galilee generally, as inferior to his own town, but he would not naturally depreciate any one of them in any marked manner. But the world over, the people of contiguous towns indulge in feelings of foolish mutual contempt, and vilify each other's locality. If, therefore, we should discover that Nathanael actually belonged to the same part of Galilee with our Saviour, and especially if we should discover that he belonged to a village near to Nazareth, we should feel that his question concerning Nazareth had the appearance of the greatest possible naturalness.

Well, we turn from the first chapter of John's gospel, where Nathanael is first introduced into the history, and where he proposes his question concerning Nazareth, to the last chapter, where alone he again appears by this name, and we find that, in the most casual way, Nathanael is mentioned as belonging to " Cana of Galilee."* This was the village where Mary the mother of Jesus had friends, and where at, the wedding-feast she seemed at home.† Cana thus appears in the history as a place

* John xxi. 2. † John ii. 5.

probably not remote from Nazareth. But, further than this, Cana has been recently identified by Dr. Robinson, as only some six or seven miles distant from Nazareth. "From the Wely above Nazareth, our friend Abu Nazir pointed out to us a ruin called Kana-el-Jelil, on the Northern side of the plain el-Buttauf, about N. ½ E., from Nazareth, and not far from three hours distant."* This place, rather than Kefr Kenna, only one and a half hours from Nazareth, Robinson, from the identity of names, as well as from other considerations, accounts the Cana of the gospels.

Precisely he who asked, "Can there any good thing come out of Nazareth?" of all others whose place of residence is given in the history, was he who lived nearest to the village where Jesus was brought up, and was therefore most likely to ask just such a question. Yet the information needed to bring together the elements of probable truth, as we have seen, is furnished only in the most incidental way.

It is generally held by Biblical scholars that Nathanael was identical with the Apostle Bartholomew. And it may be worth while just to mention here, as a pleasing coincidence, which does not require exposition in a separate chapter, that while Nathanael is represented as having been found and brought to Jesus by *Philip*, the two apostles, Philip and Bartholomew, are inseparable in the catalogues given of the twelve by the Evangelists, and were probably close companions in their apostolic ministry.

* Robinson's Palestine, vol. iii. pp. 204–5.

V.

The Healing of the Paralytic and of the Infirm Man Compared.

Mark ii. 1–12; John v. 1–9.

THE miracles of Christ were acts of self-revelation. In them were exhibited the various attributes of the God-man. The Son of God came in the nature of man to perform the work of Redemption. His miracles were a part of his work. Hence they were acts of redemption, manifesting the grace and the power of the Saviour, and were typical of the full work in which man is redeemed unto God. This is most evidently true of the miracles of healing.

In two cases of miraculous healing, our Saviour gave the command, "Rise, take up thy bed and walk." The one was that of the man "sick of the palsy, which was borne of four," who was let down into our Lord's presence through the uncovered roof. This is recorded by the first three Evangelists. The other was that of the man by the pool of Bethesda, "which had an infirmity thirty and eight years." This is recorded by the Evangelist John. According to the Harmonists, the latter of these cures followed closely upon the former.

These cures, in their principal features, were strikingly alike. In both, Jesus issued the same injunction to the helpless invalid, and in both the grand demonstration of the reality and perfection of the cure was the man's rising from the bed, which had been the near witness and supporting companion of his helplessness, and bearing it as if in triumph away.

There is, however, a difference in the accounts of the two cases, which, although at first sight apparently casual, yet upon closer consideration is found to have an instructive meaning. In the one case, the narrative states, that at the command of Christ, "immediately he arose, took up the bed, and went forth before them all." In the other case, the language is, "And immediately the man was made whole, and took up his bed and walked."

Thus it would seem that the Paralytic was not cured, in whole or in part, and of course had no evidence within himself of being cured, until he actually complied with the Saviour's command. Life came into his palsied frame and limbs, in the endeavor to rise and walk. But the Infirm man, if we may closely follow the record, was first healed, even as he lay; and having some evidence of the reality of his cure already in possession, was encouraged to try his new strength in obeying the Saviour's command, thus receiving confirmation of the reality of his cure.

Thus interpreting the records, we may, by an inspection of the full narrative in each case, perceive a difference in the *circumstances* of the two cures, admirably corresponding to the difference in the cures themselves.

The Paralytic belonged to Capernaum, the Galilean home of Jesus, one of those cities in which he performed "most of his mighty works." The previous narrative shows that already Jesus had wrought in this vicinity miracles of healing, and that just now his ministry was attended by enthusiastic multitudes. Evidently the sick man, and his friends who brought him to Jesus, had knowledge of these miracles, and had faith in Christ's gracious power. The invalid himself may have been oppressed with desponding doubts concerning the *willingness* of Christ to heal one so unworthy as himself, but these doubts must have speedily given way under the inspiring words of the Master, "Son, be of good cheer; thy sins be forgiven thee." (Matthew.) It was not until after this indication of the Saviour's merciful disposition and divine authority, and not until after the explicit assertion of his authority against the scribes present who were disposed to question it; it was not indeed until after he had given distinct intimation that he was about to heal the Paralytic by a word, and expectation, in the whole assembly and in the bosom of the invalid himself, was roused to the highest pitch of eagerness, that Jesus gave the command, "Rise, take up thy bed and walk." The narrative runs as follows: "Whether is it easier to say to the sick of the palsy, Thy sins be forgiven thee; or to say, Arise, take up thy bed and walk? But that ye may know that the Son of man hath power on earth to forgive sins, (he saith to the sick of the palsy) I say unto thee, Arise, and take up thy bed, and go thy way into thine house."

Thus, in the case of the Paralytic, a sufficient basis for active faith already existed, in the full acquaintance of the man with the Saviour; and the word of command carrying with it the strong assurance that healing would come in the very effort to obey, the man had sufficient encouragement to make the effort, even in advance of all signs that the cure had begun.

The Infirm man, on the other hand, belonged to Jerusalem. He lay in one of the porches of the pool of

Bethesda, "by the sheep-gate." And Jesus had been but little in the sacred city. He was little known there. This man might possibly have heard of the Galilean prophet, but even if so, he did not now recognize Jesus as he. Even after his cure, he "wist not who it was" that had healed him. Thus there was no basis for faith in the command of Christ, "Rise, take up thy bed and walk." Such a command, unattended by any evidence of its divine authority, must have seemed a mockery, and the poor man, wounded in spirit, would have refused any attempted compliance with it. There must, indeed, have been something in the question of Jesus, and in his whole bearing toward the invalid, adapted to win his attention. Yet, when the great Physician, drawn to that place of suffering, as we may suppose, through his unceasing sympathy for stricken humanity, and selecting the person whose case was probably most pitiable of all, and whose spiritual condition in all likelihood was best adapted to receive a saving blessing from the Redeemer's gracious interposition—when Jesus approached the poor man with the strange question, "Wilt thou be made whole?" the answer is not that of kindled expectation, as though relief were at hand, nor are the regards of the man fixed upon his questioner, as though *he* could do him any good. His reply is that of the long disappointed invalid, cherishing only a bare hope that at some time the waters of this pool may yet be his cure. He says, "Sir, I have no man, when the water is troubled, to put me into the pool; but while I am coming, another steppeth down before me." And, in immediate connection with this desponding reply, Jesus bids him rise and walk.

No wonder, then, that the record runs, *first*, "and immediately the man was made whole," and *secondly*, "and took up his bed and walked." The miracle was wrought *before* the man attempted obedience. In the absence of other means of faith, he first had evidence of Christ's power in himself, and acted upon that. He *felt* the sudden incoming of strength, the joyful tides of a new life, and *herein* recognizing the divine authority of him who spoke, leaped to obey him.

And even thus, it may be said, there are differences in the methods of grace, whereby men, helpless in sin, are brought to the enjoyment of spiritual strength. He who has been educated amidst Christian influences, has acquired a knowledge of divine truth, and has become familiar by observation with God's miracle of conversion, is commonly required to assume the vows of the Christian profession, and commence openly the Christian life, without any previous assurance of a change of heart. Taking God at his word, confiding in the promise that strength shall be equal to the day, and actually undertaking the discharge of Christian duty, assurance comes to such an one in these very efforts. Thus his conversion is like the healing of the Paralytic.

On the other hand, he who being greatly ignorant of religious things is called by God's grace into the Christian life, not unfrequently has, at the outset, a marked experience of divine power in his heart. He feels differently, and hence acts differently. His eyes are opened, his ears are unstopped, his soul is melted, and he moves forward under the impulses of the new life throbbing within him. Thus his conversion is like the healing of the Infirm man.

VI.

The Woman who was a Sinner, and Christ's Gracious Invitation.

Luke vii. 36–50; Matt. xi. 28–30.

WHO was this woman, and how came she to act in the manner described?

By many persons it is assumed that the woman who here anointed the feet of our Saviour, was none other than Mary Magdalene. And this woman being represented as formerly a notoriously dissolute person, "a sinner," this is the character popularly ascribed to Mary. Hence the name "Magdalen," commonly applied to vile women who have become penitent, and to the institutions devoted to their reformation.

There is, however, no evidence that Mary Magdalene was such a person. True, her name appears in Luke's gospel soon after this scene of the anointing.* Yet the names of other women are given along with hers, "Joanna, the wife of Chuza," and "Susanna." And the reason assigned for these women, Mary included, having attached themselves to the company of Christ, is not the reason which the Saviour's gracious treatment of "the sinner" would have supplied, but the fact that they had been "healed of evil spirits and infirmities." These women, too, "ministered unto him of their substance;" they were women of wealth and social position, which ill

* Luke viii. 2.

accords with the supposition that any of them had been women of the town.

It is indeed said of Mary Magdalene, just in this place, that out of her "went seven devils;" yet this does not argue her previous dissolute character; for possession was more nearly allied to disease and insanity, than to moral impurity. This may be inferred not only from general statements of the gospel writers, but also from specific cases. For example, the demoniac boy, whom the disciples could not relieve, had suffered a dreadful possession from his very childhood.* Of course, the idea of a previous dissolute life is here precluded.

Is it not time that intelligent readers of the gospels had dismissed from their minds all association of the Magdalene with the depraved of her sex?

But this anointing, recorded by Luke, is often confounded with another, mentioned by the other Evangelists, in which Mary of Bethany is the actor.† The reasons for imagining these to be the same, frequently given, are the following: First, the close general similarity between them; Secondly, the fact that, in both instances, the host is named Simon; and, Thirdly, the fact that, in both instances, offence is taken at the conduct of the woman.

To this it may be replied, First, that in the course of the three years of our Saviour's ministry, some similar events might very naturally occur. We know that there were two similar miracles of feeding the multitudes, and two of taking great draughts of fishes, and that on two occasions the Pharisees demanded of Christ a sign from heaven, in both of which he replied to them in the same way. Further, there are important differences in the

* Mark ix. 21. † Matt. xxvi. 6–13, and parallels.

two anointings. They differ in the time and the place of their occurrence; the evidences all going to show that this, recorded by Luke, occurred in a city of Galilee—probably Capernaum—and in the midst of our Lord's ministry, while that recorded by the others occurred at Bethany, near the close of his ministry. Moreover, nothing can be argued from the identity of the names of the hosts; for Simon was one of the most common of names, there being two Simons, for example, in the little company of the Twelve. Besides, these Simons are distinguished from each other, the one being Simon "the Pharisee," and the other Simon "the leper." Still further, while, in both instances, offence was taken at the act of anointing, it was by different persons in the two cases, here by the Pharisee, there by Christ's own disciples.

Indeed, the idea of Christ being familiarly entertained by a Pharisee at Bethany, on the eve of his crucifixion, is preposterous. Who can imagine that, when the malignity of the Pharisees had been intensified to the utmost, and was impatiently awaiting its opportunity to murder Jesus; this malignity, too, having reached its last degree of exasperation by the miracle of raising Lazarus from the dead, our Saviour should have been found publicly feasting with the Pharisees, in the immediate neighborhood of Jerusalem, with Lazarus as a prominent fellow-guest? Yet this we must believe, if we regard the two accounts of the anointing as relating to the same occurrence.

Evidently the supper at Bethany was of a simple sort. The scene is domestic; the guests are a few devoted disciples; the entertainers are friends of Jesus. The dinner at the Pharisee's house was different in all these respects.

If this reasoning be conclusive, we are relieved from the otherwise necessary yet startling inference, that the gentle Mary of Bethany had been a woman of infamous reputation.*

The way is now prepared for bringing together the two passages referred to at the outset. The illustration which is thereby secured, is the more deeply impressive, regarding the nameless woman who here exhibits such depth of contrition and such tenderness of devotion, as not Mary Magdalene, not Mary of Bethany, but as one appearing now for the first time in the history, and then lost wholly from view.

The conduct of the woman does not need to be described. The graphic language of the Evangelist sets before our eyes a full and vivid picture. "And behold, a woman in the city, which was a sinner, when she knew that Jesus sat at meat in the Pharisee's house, brought an alabaster box of ointment, and stood at his feet behind him weeping, and began to wash his feet with tears, and did wipe them with the hairs of her head, and kissed his feet, and anointed them with the ointment."

At first, the Saviour does not seem to heed this conduct, either to approve or disapprove it. In silence he permits the woman to make her heart's offering, in her chosen way; permits her to satisfy her own sweet will. And it is enough for her that she is unrebuked. The strong and affectionate desire to honor her Lord, will not be discouraged by anything short of positive prohibition.

---

* The author of the "Prince of the House of David" might well have spared himself a silly invention on this point.

Presently, when occasion offers, Jesus evinces his delighted approbation. He welcomes all that she has done, as loving evidence of her true faith. And he gives her an abundant reward for her work of love, in the assurance that her many sins are all forgiven, and in his benediction of peace.

Now, in reading this narrative, we can hardly help endeavoring to conjecture the way by which this woman had been brought to such an acquaintance with the Saviour, as led her to act in the manner described. She must at some time have attended on his personal ministry. And so doing, what gracious words must she have heard, what exhibitions of Divine compassion witnessed, and what inspirations of blessed hope enjoyed, to bring her to his feet thus dissolved in penitence and love!

But *when* had she thus been won from the ways of sin, and made a true disciple? *When* had she been brought to the step of decision, and notwithstanding all her oppressive sense of dreadful guilt, and all her apprehensions that the might and mercy of the Saviour might not reach even to her, ventured to think of him as her loving Redeemer? What was the special *occasion*—what the exhibition of Christ's unlimited power, or the declaration of his universal compassion—which had ended her weary struggles, swept away all distrust, and wrought the joyful confidence that his salvation was hers?

How naturally do such questions arise! In frequent instances, similar questions can be met only by vague and worthless conjecture. And can these be any better met? We reply that they can—that they admit of an answer highly probable, and full of delightful interest.

Let us see how the answer is reached, and what it actually is.

Immediately preceding this narrative of the anointing in Luke, we have the interview with Jesus of the messengers of John the Baptist, and the remarks of our Saviour thereby occasioned. Looking now to the eleventh chapter of Matthew, we find that it is mainly occupied with *the same matter*. And we find that the discourse of our Saviour there given, following the interview with the Baptist's messengers, a discourse connected in all its parts and complete as a whole, winds up with that most tender of all the entreaties of Divine compassion—which has therefore obtained the appellation of the Saviour's "Gracious Invitation"—"Come unto me all ye that labor and are heavy laden, and I will give you rest."* Now Luke, who gives only a portion of the

---

* Not only is there a close connection *in thought*, in all this discourse, which some would be ready to ascribe to the happy arrangement of the Evangelist, rather than to the Saviour's actual utterance, but there are *notes of time* in the transitions from one portion of the discourse to another, which determine the arrangement as that of the speaker rather than the writer. Thus we have, at the 20th verse, "Then began he;" and, at the 25th verse, "At that time Jesus answered."

The objection that portions of this discourse are represented by Luke as having been spoken at a time subsequent to this (Luke x. 13–22) amounts to nothing. These reflections of Jesus were doubtless frequently indulged, and might very naturally be repeatedly uttered.

We find ALFORD writing thus: "The whole chapter stands in such close connection, one part arising out of another, and all pervaded by the same great undertone, which sounds forth in vv. 28–30, that it is quite impossible that this should be a collection of our Lord's sayings uttered at different times." Thus also STIER: "What St. Matthew communicates in this entire chapter, is a progressive series of sayings, spoken in continuation, just as they are here connected; and forming one great concerted discourse, gradually advancing towards its climax, which in vv. 27–30, gives the most complete answer to the question which had been received."

Saviour's discourse, omitting the Gracious Invitation, records next, and as if occurring immediately upon the close of this discourse, the entrance of Jesus into the Pharisee's house, and his anointing by this woman who was a sinner. Thus, when we harmonize the narrative, the words of the Gracious Invitation are seen to be the last which Jesus publicly uttered, before taking his place at the Pharisee's table.*

Does it not hence appear in the highest degree probable, that what decided this woman, bringing her to full and happy faith, was this discourse of the Saviour, and especially its closing invitation of Divine mercy; and that she went from hearing and receiving that invitation into the Pharisee's house, to declare, in the affecting manner described, her newly inspired devotion?

And thus was this poor woman, this outcast and desolate one, the first, in the long list of the burdened and broken-hearted, whom these precious words have reached, and rescued from despair, and brought to the fulness of Divine hope.

* See Robinson's Harmony.

VII.

Sudden Outbreak of Pharisaic Hostility; and its Immediate Occasion.

Matt. xii. 24-37, and parallel passages.

ONE of the most noticeable features in the gospel history, is the growth of Pharisaic hatred and opposition, corresponding to the growth of Christ's popularity and the extension of his influence.

Jerusalem was the stronghold of Pharisaism. Our Lord began his formal public labors in Jerusalem and its vicinity, but owing to the jealousy of the Pharisees soon withdrew from Judea to remoter Galilee.*

Yet, even in Galilee, he was soon waited on and watched, not only by resident Pharisees, but by those delegated for the purpose and sent down from Jerusalem.† Such a delegation witnessed the miracle here recorded,—that of casting out the devil, blind and dumb,—and led in the ensuing conversation.‡

The hostility of the Pharisees, before this miracle was wrought, had become well pronounced. Yet never had it made such exhibition of itself as it now made. Here was a sudden outburst of opposition, not indeed in any form of physical violence, yet in a form none the less expressive of malignant desperation. It makes hot and

* John iv. 3; 43-45.   † Luke v. 17.
‡ Mark iii. 22, compared with Matt. and Luke.

energetic effort for the immediate and total destruction of our Saviour's influence over the people. These Pharisees, having witnessed the amazing miracle, in which a demoniac was healed by the power of Jesus, and being unable to deny the fact of a miracle, account for it by declaring that Jesus is in league with Beelzebub, the Prince of the devils. They seek to overwhelm him, by the confident ascription to him of such odious and diabolic character, as must have caused all who credited them to shrink from him with horror. Their device is itself characterized by diabolic ingenuity.

And as the malignant hatred of these Pharisees is thus suddenly roused, and is precipitated upon the unoffending and holy One, performing a most gracious work of healing, so, as we might well have imagined, *his spirit* is stirred to oppose his enemies with a vehemence of argument and a solemnity of warning, never before exhibited. Having shown in a happy rejoinder, that Satan cannot cast out Satan, and that if *he* may rightly be charged with having an unclean spirit, so may their own admired exorcists, he turns their minds to the consequences of their rejecting him, bringing to them as he does the kingdom of God, and declares the terrible doom of those who blaspheme against the Holy Ghost.*

The question occurs, what was it that, *on this occasion*, aroused the fierce opposition of the enemies of Jesus? Cures of demoniacs had before been wrought by the

---

* How deeply the heart of Jesus was grieved by this vile charge of his enemies, we might infer from the way in which he recalled and signalized it, on the occasion of his sending forth the Twelve. "If they have called the Master of the house Beelzebub, how much more shall they call them of his household." Matt. x. 25.

Saviour. And, as the whole history shows, he had recently performed other miracles, in great number and variety, in circumstances of greater or less publicity. It is hardly satisfactory to suppose that the mere performance of an additional similar miracle should, of itself, have occasioned this outburst of vindictive passion.

The clue to an explanation completely satisfactory is given by Matthew, in a statement omitted by those other evangelists who narrate the charge of the Pharisees. It is the statement that, in view of this miracle, "all the people were amazed, and said, Is not this *the Son of David?*"

This quiet statement may be easily passed over, in a hurried reading, without a thought of its peculiar significance. "The Son of David," imports nothing less than the long looked-for Messiah, the mighty Deliverer of Israel. And the question, whether Jesus is not he, now eagerly and expectantly asked, shows that the multitudes in attendance on the ministry of Jesus, and witnesses of the miracle just wrought, were rapidly coming to the belief that Jesus was the Messiah.

Not long before this, as the Harmonists show, Jesus had raised to life the son of the widow of Nain. And in connection with that miracle, as we are told, "there came a fear on all; and they glorified God, saying, That a great Prophet is risen up among us; and that God hath visited his people. And this rumor of him went forth throughout all Judea, and throughout all the region round about."* That miracle evidently produced a new impression, concerning the person who was performing these marvellous works. He was assuredly God's own mighty

* Luke vii. 16, 17.

messenger—perhaps the Messiah himself. And this new impression became widely prevalent.

Directly after this, it would appear, John sent his messengers to Jesus, inquiring "Art thou he that should come, or look we for another?" Art thou indeed the Messiah? And the answer and discourse of Jesus, following upon this, must have tended to confirm the popular impression previously received, and to lead the people to think, even more distinctly than before, that Jesus might be the Messiah.

And now, when a new miracle is wrought before their eyes, in which, by a single exertion of the power of Jesus, a demon is expelled, the dumb is made to speak, and the blind to see, the people, previously excited to eager expectation, can no longer refrain from expressing their ardent hope, and they pass round the earnest inquiry, "Is not this the Son of David?" Must he not be, in very truth, our Messiah? "When Messias cometh, will he do more miracles than this man doeth?" And probably the popular excitement, rapidly kindled, was just ready to break forth in mighty conflagration.

And hence the vigorous promptness of the interposition of the Pharisees. The popular acknowledgment of Jesus as the Messiah would be fatal to their power. He would sweep away the whole existing order of things. An emergency has arisen, and they bestir themselves to meet it. They rush to the rescue. They stamp upon the kindling sparks, and repress the rising flames. Thus it is that the narrative runs, "But when the Pharisees *heard it*"—heard that thrilling question, "Is not this the Son of David?"—"they said," thus and so, casting upon Jesus their vile imputation.

And see how admirably their course meets the exigency. The people are ascribing to Jesus the most exalted character. They are viewing him as the powerful messenger of the Most High God. And the Pharisees cry, "He is indeed great in power, but not as the ally of the Lord. The mightier he is, the more is he to be dreaded. He casts out devils, because leagued with the Prince of the Devils."*

Thus we see that just such occasion was offered these Pharisees, as was required in order that they should naturally have acted precisely as they did. And it may not be amiss to suggest further, that in all probability the efforts of the Pharisees were, for a time and to a degree, successful. The minds of the people were diverted from their previous thoughts, and the subsequent history leads us to think, that, under the specious and confident calumnies of their revered religious teachers, doubts came upon many concerning the character of Jesus.†

---

* In Matt. ix. 27-34, we have a brief record concerning two miracles; the first, of the healing of two blind men who followed him, crying, "Thou Son of David, have mercy on us;" the second, of the dispossession of a dumb demoniac, to the great astonishment of the multitudes, and to the exasperation of the Pharisees, who said, "He casteth out devils, through the Prince of the Devils." These miracles, although presented in the record prior to the miracle under consideration, are commonly regarded by the Harmonists as having actually occurred after it, the account of them being placed next after that of the raising of the daughter of Jairus. The order as given by Matthew, is, however, followed by some. LANGE, *in loco*, referring to Matt. ix. 34, says, "The former *private* accusation, that Jesus was in league with Satan, was now publicly and boldly brought forward."

† It may be seen that after this the element of admonition becomes more prominent in the Saviour's teachings. He warns the people against rejecting himself, cautions them against the influence of the Pharisees, and

It is interesting, moreover, to observe, how, in other instances, Pharisaic hatred to Jesus exploded, upon the ascription to him of the Messianic character, under this same appellation, "Son of David."

On the occasion of his triumphal entry into Jerusalem, when the people were bestowing this title upon him in their Hosannas, we read that "some of the Pharisees from among the multitude said unto him, Master, rebuke thy disciples." And shortly after, when, in the temple, the children took up the cry, " Hosanna to the Son of David," the record is that the chief priests and scribes "were sore displeased, and said unto him, Hearest thou what these say?"

Thus we have a glimpse of Pharisaic hostility, when Jesus was in the midst of his Galilean ministry. This opposition was afterward still more fully organized, and made still more formidable. The subsequent history shows the Saviour in perpetual view of it, and in frequent conflict with it. For a long time he completely baffles it. At last, his active ministry having been accomplished, and his hour fully come, a disciple betrays him to these enemies, and he yields himself to their murderous will, in the exclamation, "Now is your hour and the power of darkness."

denounces the Pharisees themselves. Also, when our Saviour afterward asked his disciples, "Who do men say that I, the Son of Man, am?" (Matt. xvi. 13,) amidst the great variety of opinions stated in reply, as held by the people, nothing is said of the opinion being entertained by any that he was the Messiah.

VIII.

Levi's Feast, in several relations; especially Christ's Representation of Himself as the Bridegroom.

Matt. ix. 15, and parallels; also John iii. 29.

A STUDY of the simple narrative of the "reception"* given to the Saviour by Levi, (whom we regard as identical with Matthew,) where the Master ate with publicans and sinners, shows this portion of the history, in the different parts of it, linked in with the history elsewhere, in a very remarkable manner. No inventor of history has been equal to the work of producing a narrative so vividly natural as this, and at the same time of so inserting it into a body of history, as to give it living relations to every portion. This brief section is a tree which sends its roots deep and wide into the whole soil of the evangelic narratives.

We may only glance at a few of the instances which illustrate this, reserving special remark for the representation above announced of Christ as the Bridegroom.

In the first place, as has frequently been observed, we have an evidence of naturalness in the fact that while it is Matthew who gives the feast, and while Mark informs us that the feast was given at Matthew's house, and while Luke declares that it was "a great feast," made at Matthew's "own house," Matthew him-

* Luke.

self, in his account of it, modestly conceals the fact that it was a feast, and that it was given by himself and at his own house, simply saying, "And it came to pass, as Jesus sat at meat in the house."

Again: On this occasion, Jesus mingles with outcasts from Jewish society, doing so for their spiritual benefit, going among them as a physician among the sick. Evidently from this, the Saviour regarded the publicans and their companions as most hopeful subjects of his ministry. And how exactly and remarkably does this judgment of the Saviour coincide with the intimations of the history given elsewhere. Thus we find the publicans frequenting John's baptism: "Then came also publicans to be baptized, and said unto him, Master, what shall we do?"* Also we find that the reception of John's ministry by the publicans was of so marked and suitable a sort, as to be particularly mentioned in the subsequent history. In connection with Christ's encomium on the Baptist, it is said that "all the people that heard him, *and the publicans,* justified God, being baptized with the baptism of John."† And far on in the history, at a time long subsequent to Matthew's feast, we hear our Saviour addressing the chiefs of the nation in these emphatic words, "Verily I say unto you, that the publicans and harlots go into the kingdom of God before you."‡

The facts on this subject, disclosed in the most casual way at different times, yet exactly agreeing with one another, are these: First, By the Baptist's ministry, the publicans and their associates had been brought into a condition to make Christ's labors among them most

* Luke iii. 12.   † Luke vii. 29.   ‡ Matt. xxi. 31.

hopeful. Next, one well-known publican soon became an apostle, and Christ, by his agency, comes into near contact with the whole class of his fellows, preaching to them the kingdom of God. And lastly, the members of this class are found entering the ranks of Christ's followers, when others were steadily refusing discipleship.

Again: In immediate connection with this feast, a deputation waited on our Lord, proposing to him an important question. From Luke's account, we should have inferred that this deputation consisted only of Scribes and Pharisees; for Luke, having spoken of these before, continues his narrative as follows, "And *they* said unto him." From Matthew we should have inferred that the deputation consisted only of certain adherents of the Baptist; for Matthew's language is, "Then came to him *the disciples of John,* saying," etc. The apparent discrepancy, which in other similar instances can commonly be reconciled by reasonable conjecture, is here reconciled by Mark's statement, that "the disciples of John *and* of the Pharisees" "come and say unto him." These two parties unite in their mission, having alike been accustomed *to fast*, their question relating mainly to fasting.

Now how natural that the inquiry, "Why do the disciples of John and of the Pharisees fast, but thy disciples fast not?" should have been made in connection with a *feast;* how true is the information here given to what we know elsewhere of John's *ascetic* character; and how exactly was the contrast hereby presented between the conduct of John and of Christ, in the malignant view taken of it by the Pharisees, expressed by the Saviour, when he said, "For John the Baptist came neither eating bread nor drinking wine, and ye say, He hath a devil. The Son of man is come eating and drinking, and ye say: Behold a gluttonous man and a wine-bibber, a friend of publicans and sinners."*

Again: In Luke's account of the question of this deputation, we find proposed not only the matter of fasting, but also of praying. Luke writes, "Why do the disciples of John fast often, and *make prayers?*" From this it is evident, that the Baptist prescribed rigid rules not only concerning fasting, but also concerning praying. It seems natural to infer that he gave them some formularies of prayer. And how exactly, yet how wholly incidentally, is this inference established by the direct narrative elsewhere. Thus it is said, "And it came to pass that as he was praying in a certain place, when he ceased, one of his disciples said unto him, Lord, teach us to pray, *as John also taught his disciples*."† And it was on this occasion that, for the second time, the Master gave that formulary commonly known as "The Lord's Prayer."‡

---

* Luke vii. 33, 34. † Luke xi. 1.

‡ We have omitted to compare this instance in which our Saviour ate with publicans and sinners, with that in which he became the guest of Zaccheus the publican, or as his enemies phrased it, "guest with a man that is a sinner." (Luke xix. 2–10.) The comparison will be found instructive.

Also, we have not called attention to the saying of Christ, quoted from the Old Testament, "I will have mercy and not sacrifice," applied here, and also on another occasion. (Matthew xii. 7.) It may be seen that the saying has an application equally apt in the two instances. Also, regarding Levi's Feast as having occurred *after* the plucking of the ears of corn on the Sabbath, as the Harmonists show to have been probable, we perceive the reason of Christ's greater severity of rebuke, when now

We come now to our Saviour's reply to the question of this deputation, in which is found the figure of the bridegroom. He justifies the absence of fasting, in the case of his disciples, on the ground that the present is with them a time of joy. The general teaching is, that fasting may not properly be observed for its own sake, and without regard to seasons and circumstances. Fasting is suitable for the time of mourning, and is becoming to the disciples of Christ whenever he is not joyfully manifest to them; but fasting in circumstances of joy is incongruous and undesirable.

This teaching our Saviour clothes in figurative language. He asks, "Can the children of the bride-chamber"—the near attendants of the bridegroom—can they "mourn, as long as the bridegroom is with them?" —while the marriage festivities continue? "But the days will come, when the bridegroom shall be taken from them, and then shall they fast." This figure was, of course, perfectly intelligible and highly forcible, in itself considered; weddings, by universal agreement, being accounted and celebrated as joyful occasions. And the Saviour's language affords a complete and satisfactory reply to the immediate question of both John's disciples and the Pharisees concerning fasting. Yet, when we bring into connection with this passage that found in John iii. 29, and regard our Saviour as now tacitly referring to that passage, in his use of the figure of the bridegroom, his reply becomes, for the adherents of John, not only far more forcible, but far more widely

---

making this quotation. His enemies had been *slow* to learn the lesson which he had once before given them. And he will have them now "go" instantly, "and learn what that meaneth."

reaching. This point, we think, deserves a careful examination.

The Baptist's disciples, on the occasion referred to, had been discussing with the Jews some questions concerning purifications.* Just as here, they were troubled about the outward rites of religion. And evidently their discussion with the Jews had something to do with the right of Christ's disciples to baptize, which the latter were now doing; for to this they make distinct reference. Alarmed at the growing popularity of Jesus, and the corresponding decline of the cause of their own Master, they come to John with the complaint, "Rabbi, he that was with thee beyond Jordan, to whom thou barest witness, behold, the same baptizeth, and all men come to him." And the Baptist, in reply, nobly avowed that this state of things was every way suitable. He reasserts his own humble character, as the mere harbinger of the Messiah. He ascribes to Jesus a character infinitely superior to his own. Jesus has come from above, and is above all, while *he* is only of the earth, and speaks of the earth. And as Jesus is infinitely superior to him in character and authority, it is fitting that the ministry of Christ should engage supreme attention, and that his own ministry should be disregarded and forsaken, for "He must increase, but I must decrease."

It is in the midst of such statements as these, that the Baptist introduces the figure of the Bridegroom, applying it to Jesus and himself. "He that hath the bride, is the bridegroom; but the friend of the bridegroom, which standeth and heareth him, rejoiceth greatly

* See John iii. 25–34.

because of the bridegroom's voice; this my joy therefore is fulfilled."

When, then, John's disciples come to Jesus with a question about rites and forms, dissatisfied that Jesus does not insist on the same outward observances which their Master had required, being thus disposed to adhere to John as against Jesus; and when, in reply to them, Jesus uses the same figure of speech which had afforded the central and governing thought in that discourse of the Baptist in which *he* had settled these matters for his disciples; can we help thinking that the Saviour *adopted* the figure—*intended* the coincidence—and meant to bring the authority of the Baptist to bear upon his dissatisfied disciples?

Thus Christ seems to say to them, "Your own Master taught you that I am the bridegroom, to stand in whose presence is a joy. If this be so, can my disciples, children of the bridechamber, living in my joyful presence, do otherwise than rejoice? And, further, why do you not acquiesce in my authority, even though my rules of discipline be different from those of John, when he taught you that he was only my servant, and that my authority was law to himself? And still further, why adhere to John as against me, placing yourselves now in the company of opposing Pharisees, when your Master so plainly taught you that his ministry was only intended to usher in mine, and that none could properly join themselves to him, except for the end of becoming my disciples?"

Thus bringing these two passages together, our Saviour's language, in the instance before us, is clothed with a far wider and fuller meaning. And that our

Saviour intended his saying to be viewed in the light of that of his Forerunner, seems evident from the exact harmony subsisting between them, at so many points, and from the fitness of their concurrence to his purpose. Yet the two are not brought together by the Evangelists. The coincidence seems to have been on their part undesigned.

IX.

The Disciples unexpectedly compelled to Embark and Cross the Lake: and the Reason for it.

Matt. xiv. 22. John vi. 14, 15.

THE Apostles had returned from their trial mission, and made report concerning it to the Master. Upon his proposition, they took ship with him for the farther side of the sea of Galilee, to avoid the multitudes, and secure rest and leisure, at least sufficient for an undisturbed meal. "And the Apostles gathered themselves together unto Jesus, and told him all things, both what they had done and what they had taught. And he said unto them, Come ye yourselves apart into a desert place, and rest a while: for there were many coming and going, and they had no leisure so much as to eat."*

With this movement, the intelligence just received, of the beheading of John the Baptist, also had something to do.†

The multitudes, however, anticipated this movement, and anxious to continue in the Saviour's company, they made their way by land around the head of the lake, and were ready to meet him when he disembarked. Jesus compassionately renews among them his ministry, both of preaching and of healing their sick, and, doubtless, the previous admiration for him suffers no abate-

* Mark vi. 30, 31. † Matt. xiv. 13.

ment, but corresponding increase. These multitudes, consisting largely of people from the country, now on their way to the passover, were probably less influenced by the hostile Pharisees, and were more ready to yield their tribute of praise to Jesus, than were the inhabitants of Capernaum.*

As the day wears away, and the necessity for something to eat becomes pressing, Jesus performs that astounding miracle, in which five loaves and two fishes are multiplied into sufficient food for the many thousands.

Immediately after this, we find that Jesus, instead of withdrawing from the multitudes with his disciples, in order that they may quietly remain together in that retired place, according to their intention in coming there, —instead of this, compels his disciples to take again to their vessel and return across the lake, while he remains to dismiss the multitudes. (Matt. and Mark.)

This, even upon the most casual view, seems strange; yet, when we examine the language of the record, it is still more surprising. Both writers use the same words. They say that "*straightway*," he "*constrained*" his disciples to get into the ship. His act was prompt and authoritative. It compelled a reluctant obedience. Evidently a crisis of some sort had suddenly arisen. Evidently the disciples were now involved in some matter or movement unwelcome to the Master. Evidently they were so much in earnest in it, and so determined upon it, that only the most decisive measures on his part were adequate to suppress it.

But where else are any intimations of such a crisis

* John vi. 4. See also page 47.

having come, or of anything unusual having occurred involving the disciples? No such intimations are found elsewhere in the two gospels quoted. And none are to be found, so far as we know, anywhere else, save in the parallel account in John's gospel. That account does not, indeed, say a word concerning Christ's compelling his disciples to leave the place. The disciples are not so much as mentioned. Yet John's account of what occurred immediately after the miracle, is found to *supplement* that of Matthew and Mark, and the two together furnish the materials with which to reproduce an extraordinary scene, otherwise not dreamed of, enacted just at that time, on the banks of the sea of Galilee.

We cannot but think that the effect of such a miracle as that of feeding the five thousand men, not only witnessed, but actually participated in, by those who were already aroused to high enthusiasm, would be well nigh overwhelming. And the statement of John, although very simple, is immensely significant. He writes, "Then those men, when they had seen the miracle that Jesus did, said, This is of a truth that Prophet that should come into the world." They settled it in their minds, and proclaimed it to one another, that Jesus was the long-predicted prophet like unto Moses. Diseases have fled at his touch, and now bread for thousands has issued from his creative hands, and herein they see God visiting his people and removing from them the curse. And if Jesus shall have sway, there will be no more sickness, no more poverty, no more toil; all want and woe will disappear. Probably they think that if he be indeed "that Prophet," he must be the promised "Son of David," and hence their desires seem to them to conspire with God's purposes, when they cry, "Come, let us make him *a king*, and join ourselves to him as his steadfast and happy subjects, and receive the blessings of his reign." For, as John further informs us, the people were ready actually to enthrone Jesus, and would have used the most energetic means to accomplish their purpose, had he not thwarted them. John writes, "When Jesus therefore perceived that they would come and take him by force, to make him a king, he departed again into a mountain himself alone."*

Thus, then, John's gospel shows the *people* in a state of intense excitement, just ready to enthrone the Saviour, and the Saviour watching the unwelcome movement and taking measures to thwart it; while Matthew and Mark show us the *disciples* suddenly compelled by the Master to embark upon their vessel, and quit the scene of the miracle and the multitudes.

It needs no great effort of the imagination to combine these representations. We know well enough that the disciples could not have been indifferent spectators of what was going on among the people. We know well enough that they would be little likely to use their influence in quelling the excitement and restraining the proposed movement. The narratives elsewhere give us abundant evidence of the worldly views of the disciples concerning the Messiah and his kingdom. They could not brook the thought that the Master should realize his predicted character of a suffering Saviour.† They were

---

* The supposition is not improbable that as the multitude were on the way to the passover, they intended to conduct Jesus in triumph to Jerusalem, and enthrone him there.

† See Ch. III. p. 21.

eager for positions of worldly honor in the coming kingdom.* Even after the Resurrection, and just before the Ascension, they hoped that Jesus would even then assume the throne of David and restore the power of the Jewish nation.†

Is it not, indeed, in the highest degree probable, that now the disciples fully shared the feelings of the people? May we not think that, at the suggestion of the people, they headed the movement in hand? Were they not the ringleaders in this project of enthroning their Master; a project intended to honor him, yet wholly mistaken, unworthy, and destructive of his plans, and demanding from him the most prompt and vigorous efforts to crush it?‡

Nothing can be more natural than these suggestions. Yet they enable us to complete the picture of that scene in which Jesus resists the efforts of the people to enthrone him. For they show the Saviour seizing upon his disciples, tearing them from the multitudes, sending them to their ship, and commanding them away, as the most direct and effective method of breaking the popular spell, and hindering the popular design.

No wonder that the disciples yielded to the Master most unwillingly. No wonder that his full authority was needed in order to resist them. They were relinquishing the present fulfillment of their most fondly an-

---

* See Ch. XVI. † Acts i. 6.

‡ DA COSTA, writing upon another subject, calls attention to the fact, that Mark here uses a *military* word, and that the accurate translation would here be, "while he *disbanded* the multitudes." This looks as if the people had already *organized* themselves for the intended effort.
See "The Four Witnesses," p. 100.

ticipated schemes. They were consenting to see their most ardently cherished hopes yet longer deferred.

Need we marvel, in view of all the probabilities, that the record runs, "And straightway Jesus constrained his disciples to get into a ship, and to go before him unto the other side, while he sent the multitudes away?" This declaration, rather, is seen to meet the exact and full state of the case, as all the probabilities represent it.

X.

Crisis in the History of Judas.

John vi. 70, 71.

THIS chapter needs to be considered in connection with the preceding.

The next day after the miracle of feeding the five thousand men, Jesus is found in the Synagogue of Capernaum. His disciples are with him, and many of those who, the day before, had shared in his miraculous bounty, and sought to enthrone him as the Messiah. Likewise hostile "Jews" are present, at first retired and silent, but soon coming conspicuously forward.

In answer to the question of curiosity, asked by some who had been with him the previous evening, "Rabbi, when camest thou hither?" Jesus commences a discourse of the highest practical moment. He at once rebukes the worldly spirit of his auditors, and directs their attention to himself as a spiritual rather than a worldly benefactor. "Jesus answered them and said, Verily, verily, I say unto you, Ye seek me, not because ye saw the miracles, but because ye did eat of the loaves, and were filled. Labor not for the meat which perisheth, but for that meat which endureth unto everlasting life." Thus the discourse harmonizes with his conduct the evening before, in breaking up the attempt to make him a worldly king.

The discourse, conceived in this strain, falls upon unwilling ears. Questions arise; unbelief begins its demands; and, when Jesus, instead of proffering proofs of his divine claims, proceeds to assert those claims in a manner still more offensive, the hostile Jews commence their murmurings, and from murmurings go on to a very tumult of strife. They asked, "How is it that he saith, I came down from heaven?" They "strove among themselves, saying, How can this man give us his flesh to eat."—Meanwhile Jesus only advances still more absolute claims, and asserts the truth in still more offensive forms. He is the bread of life, and except they eat the flesh of the Son of man and drink his blood, they have no life in them.

Thus does Jesus, exhibiting himself in mysterious words, as a spiritual benefactor, endeavor to cut up by the roots all mere worldly expectation concerning him.

As the result of this exposition of the Saviour's doctrine, not only were those greatly exasperated who had before been hostile to him, but many who had attached themselves to his ministry forsook him. "From that time many of his disciples went back, and walked no more with him." They were glad to share the outward advantages conferred by his miracles, but they had no faith to receive his teachings which seemed strange to the natural understanding, and they had no such spiritual desires as disposed them to embrace him as the Messiah of their hearts.

The juncture was most solemn. The chaff was rapidly separating from the wheat, the Son of man having taken his fan in hand and proceeding to purge his threshing-floor. The disappointed and offended multitudes were forsaking him; even many of those who had been his admiring followers were dropping from his presence; the contagion bids fair to become universal, and Jesus seems about to be left utterly alone. At this juncture, he turns upon the twelve, with the solemn appeal, "Will ye also go away?" The appeal does not long remain unanswered. Peter responds, for himself and his fellows, in those affecting, noble words of love and faith, "Lord, to whom shall we go? Thou hast the words of eternal life. And we believe, and are sure that thou art that Christ, the Son of the Living God."

And now come the words to which we would invite special attention. For, how does Jesus receive this confession of his disciples? We cannot but think that it must have been most grateful to him. We naturally look to see him approve and honor it. We know that when Peter made a similar confession, under circumstances much less trying, Jesus exclaimed, "Blessed art thou, Simon Bar-jona."* Yet now we find that Jesus replies to the confession of his disciples, most strangely and abruptly, with words of stern reproach and condemnation. He asks, as if in indignation, "Have not I chosen you twelve, and one of you is a devil?" And the Evangelist informs us, that "he spake of Judas Iscariot, the son of Simon; for he it was that should betray him, being one of the twelve."

Who can read this narrative, without inquiring why it was that the falseness of Judas' character should just now have risen so prominently before the mind of the Saviour as apparently to overshadow all things else?

We might at first imagine that this intense feeling of

* Matt. xvi. 16.

displeasure against Judas was now aroused, simply in view of the fact that he had hypocritically acquiesced in the solemn avowal just made of attachment to Christ, and of faith in his Messiahship. But was there not equal hypocrisy in Judas' acquiescence in the confession of Peter, referred to above? Yet, on that occasion, Jesus does not advert to this hypocrisy, but only commends his disciples? There seems to have been something peculiar in the case of Judas, just at this time.

And may there not, we ask, have been just now a marked development in the character of Judas? May not the hypocrisy of Judas, as now manifested, have been something new? May not this have been the critical occasion in which Judas passed from the condition of a self-deceived disciple, to that of a conscious hypocrite? May not Judas have shared the disappointment and disgust of the worldly multitudes and fickle followers of Jesus, and had it in his heart to leave his Master; and may he not now in heart have *actually turned from him*, so far as a true regard for him was concerned, yet have resolved to remain with him, a false friend, in the hope of some worldly advantages yet to be enjoyed?

Now this probable view is rendered almost certain, when we connect with the passage in question the considerations of the foregoing chapter.

We are to believe that Judas attached himself to the Saviour under the governing desire of sharing that worldly exaltation which he believed Jesus would soon attain. The other apostles expected such exaltation, and desired to share it; but with Judas this unworthy feeling was dominant and supreme, as it was not with the others. When, then, under the influence of the miracle of worldly blessing—the miracle of abundant food—the people prepared to enthrone Jesus as a worldly king, what a moment of exultation it must have been for Judas! Even now he beholds his cherished hopes bursting into glad fulfillment! And no doubt, if, as we have been led to think, the disciples, as a body, headed the people in their excited attempt, Judas was probably foremost in this matter among the disciples. He was *the* ringleader. His presence was everywhere seen, his voice was everywhere heard, directing his fellow-disciples and organizing the multitudes, on that memorable afternoon.

And when Jesus interfered, seizing upon the Apostles and sending them away, it must have been Judas who engaged the special attentions of the Saviour and occasioned his most authoritative efforts. More reluctantly than any of the rest would Judas cease from his attempt; more unwillingly leave the scene and retire to the vessel. And if, in the case of the others, the disappointment was keen, and well nigh overwhelming, much more would it be so with him.

No wonder, then, if, when, the next day, Jesus, in the most explicit manner, exposed the mistake of those who followed him from worldly motives, and gave them clearly to understand that he was not a worldly but a spiritual Saviour, Judas' mind was made up, and he resolved to have nothing further to do with the Saviour and his cause than might serve his personal sordid ends. And thus would the chosen disciple stand revealed to the discerning eye of the Master, as one who was not in league with himself; as one who had taken sides against him and had sold himself to the Wicked One.

The miracle and the discourse of Christ taken together, afforded the occasion which discriminated among the multitudes the true disciples from the false. And these taken together exhibit a juncture critical, in like manner, with the false Apostle. Judas, sharing with the multitudes in their expectations and their disappointment by the sea of Galilee, shared also in their disgust, and their decision against the Saviour, in the synagogue of Capernaum. Nay, if he had been the leader in the scheme to enthrone the Saviour, so may he have been foremost in the ensuing disaffection; for when, before Peter's confession, many of his disciples said, "This is an hard saying, who can hear it?" Jesus addressed the murmurers with words of admonition, adding, "but there are some of you who believe not." And the Evangelist continues, showing the prominence of Judas herein, "For Jesus knew from the beginning who they were that believed not, *and who should betray him.*"

XI.

The Person who saw Men as Trees walking not born blind.

Mark viii. 22–26; John ix.

THE incident here narrated by Mark receives illustration from that recorded by John, above referred to, as will be presently seen, only in a negative way.

The healing of the blind man at Bethsaida is distinguished from most, if not all the other miracles, by its being wrought progressively. It also involved, on the part of the Saviour, numerous and peculiar acts. Probably these peculiar acts were employed, both to show that no fixed mode was essential in the working of miracles, and also to assist the faith of the blind man, which seems to have been very weak. Those who brought the man besought Christ "to *touch* him," as though this might be the invariable or even necessary mode of performing miraculous cures; also the man is not represented as himself having faith in Jesus, but rather it is his friends, who bring him and intercede for him, whose faith appears.

The narrative of the healing is on this wise. "And he took the blind man by the hand, and led him out of the town; and when he had spit on his eyes, and put his hands upon him, he asked him if he saw aught. And he looked up, and said, '*I see men as trees walking.*'

After that, he put his hands again upon his eyes, and made him look up: and he was restored, and saw every man clearly."

The point of special interest, at present, is this; that supposing the man to have been *born* blind, it would be difficult to understand how he should be able, on first coming to sight, to judge of the comparative appearance of men and of trees, and of the proper motion of walking. It is in great measure by experience that we learn how the forms of things ought to appear. Persons born blind are sometimes brought to sight, through modern surgical skill, as in cases of congenital cataract. And it is said that the blind, coming for the first time to sight, are unable to judge of forms and distances. They cannot, simply by sight, distinguish a globe from a cube. They must *handle* these objects in connection with seeing them, in order afterward to judge of them aright upon simple sight. They have no idea of perspective, all things appearing equally near or remote; and not until they have gone freely about, is their vision competently instructed to judge of comparative distances.

We may not indeed limit a miracle. The miracle wrought by Peter and John, on the man lame from his birth, who lay "at the gate of the temple, which is called Beautiful," not only gave strength to "his feet and ancle-bones," so that he might of himself have afterwards *learned* to walk, but it also gave the skill which is usually acquired by experience, so that "he leaping up, stood, and walked, and entered with them into the temple, walking and leaping and praising God."*

* Acts iii. 2–8.

Yet, as a general fact, miracles *end* where natural causes may suitably *begin*. Thus the daughter of Jairus was brought to *life* and *health*, yet she was not miraculously *strengthened* in body. Natural food was sufficient to strengthen her, and Jesus "commanded that something should be given her to eat." In the case of the lame man just mentioned, there was a great *moral* result to be attained, in giving the miracle such extent of operation as to enable the man at once and fully to exercise his powers. It thus had an effect, which it otherwise would not have had, in testifying for the risen Saviour and his religion.

But, in the case before us, not only is there no evident reason for giving such extent to the miracle, but further, the miracle itself was not completed, when the patient "saw men as trees walking." And it does not seem natural to suppose that the miracle should have conferred the skill of experience, before it had conferred the full power of simple vision—the power to see things "clearly."

Yet the whole difficulty, be it observed, is simply one of supposition. For the narrative does *not* state nor imply that the man was *born* blind. It says nothing directly upon the subject. It does use one word, which, in an apparently undesigned way, intimates that the man was *not* born blind. It says that he "was *restored* ;" as if he had previously *lost* his vision, and had now got it back again.

Negative proof is sometimes the strongest of all proof. It is common, with the Scripture writers, to exhibit the most desperate features in the case of those on whom miracles were performed, doubtless in order that the reality and the wonderful character of the miracles might be sufficiently made evident. Thus it is stated that the infirm man at the pool of Bethesda had been afflicted thirty and eight years; that the woman with an issue of blood had suffered for twelve years, and had spent her whole living on physicians in vain; and that Lazarus had been dead four days.* And not only might we naturally suppose that it would have been a circumstance worth mentioning, if this man had been born blind, but we find that, in the case recorded in the ninth of John above cited, this fact is distinctly and repeatedly referred to, throughout the chapter, as one of the notable features of the case. The statement is not only made at the beginning of the chapter, that the man "was blind from his birth." This might have been done because of the ensuing conversation, in which Christ answered the question of his disciples, "Master, who did sin, this man or his parents, that he was born blind?" But afterward the Jews demand of the parents, "Is this your son, who ye say was *born blind?*" And the parents respond, "We know that this is our son, and that he was *born blind.*" And the man himself exclaims, "Since the world began, was it not heard that any man opened the eyes of one that was *born blind.*"

Now, how vastly easy would it have been for an inventor of history, or even for a truthful but careless historian, to have represented the man of Bethsaida as born blind, and thus unconsciously afforded the difficulty above presented. But the Scripture records are not in-

---
* John v. 5; Mark v. 25, 26; John xi. 39.

ventions; neither are they the product of mere honest blunderers. Rather they recount actual occurrences, *even when these are stupendous miracles;* and they are minutely truthful, even as such "undesigned coincidences" most forcibly testify.

XII.

The Opening of a New Era in the Ministry of Christ.
Matthew xvi. 21, and its parallels.

BY consulting the passages cited, it will be seen that our Saviour now explicitly foretold his death and resurrection. He taught "his disciples," not the people generally, that he "must suffer many things," be "rejected" by the chiefs of the nation, be put to death, and "be raised again the third day." He represented this dread consummation as awaiting him in Jerusalem, and declared that under the sublime necessity of his mission, he "must go unto Jerusalem" to meet it.

It is important to understand that this teaching was *something new* to the disciples, and further, that Jesus now began this teaching, to continue it at intervals until the predicted consummation was actually reached. Indeed, we need to understand that a *new era* in the life and ministry of our Saviour was now opening, in which his coming sufferings and death were to be held conspicuously in view, and in which his movements were to be governed, to an extent not before seen, by the anticipation of them.*

---

* BENGEL *in loco* observes, "The Gospel may be divided into two parts, from which the Divine plan of Jesus shines forth. The first proposition is, *Jesus is the Christ;* the second, *Christ must suffer, die, and rise again,* or more briefly, *Christ by death will enter into glory.* Jesus first convinced

The fact that this teaching was something new, would sufficiently appear from the language of our Saviour here employed, if we would but give his expressions their due significance. Mark writes, that "he *began* to teach them that the Son of man must suffer many things." Our Lord, before this, had given some obscure hints upon this subject, but now his teachings were clear and explicit.* This is also expressed by Mark, when he further writes, "And he spake that saying *openly*." Matthew looks to the new *era* which was now commencing, when he says, "*From that time forth* began Jesus to show unto his disciples," etc. While hitherto the subject of his passion had been referred to, only in the way of brief and casual intimations, it was now to become a frequent and prominent theme of discourse.

The fact that this teaching was new to the disciples, appears also from their manner of receiving it. It took them by surprise. It excited the profoundest emotions. It presented their Master and his mission in a strange and painful light.

We have had occasion already to observe Peter's conduct on this announcement of our Saviour; how, unable to endure it, he took the Master aside, and ventured not only to remonstrate with him but even to rebuke him.† No doubt this feeling of Peter was shared by his companions. The thought of a suffering and re-

his disciples of the first proposition; in consequence of which they were bound to believe him concerning the second, even before his passion. As soon as Jesus had persuaded his disciples of the first proposition, he added the second."

* John iii. 14. Matt. x. 38, etc. † See page 25.

jected Messiah was wholly foreign to their minds. They had been so far enlightened concerning the person of Christ, as to be able to make that confident acknowledgment of him, recorded just before Jesus began this new teaching, when, to the question of the Master, "But who do ye say that I am?" Peter answered, "Thou art the Christ, the Son of the living God." Yet they regarded Christ chiefly in the light of a prophet and of a king. They had not yet apprehended him in his priestly character.

Now, what we have said above, receives full illustration from the history. By comparing the evangelic records prior to this time, with those which follow, we may readily see that now a new chapter was opened in the ministry of Christ. We may see that the anticipation of his dreadful trials and bloody passion, not only led the Saviour, from this time forth, to speak with his disciples on this subject, in occasional and formal instructions, but also tinged his various thoughts, affected his various movements, and brought to him peculiar experiences, thus giving distinct character to his whole subsequent ministry.

It may be enough for us now, remembering the absence of explicit teachings hitherto concerning Christ's passion, to instance a few passages, in the subsequent history, in which the subject is distinctly treated.

Only a week after Jesus began this new instruction, occurred his transfiguration. In this sublime event we behold one of those peculiar experiences of the Saviour, just referred to, granted him in view of his coming humiliation. Likewise it had for the disciples an important teaching, as we shall by and by show. But in connection with this event, our Saviour is found making, to the three disciples who attended him, a distinct reference to his death and resurrection. "As they came down from the mountain, Jesus charged them, saying, Tell the vision to no man, until the Son of Man be risen again from the dead." One of the Evangelists informs us that the disciples "kept that saying with themselves, questioning one with another what the rising from the dead should mean." (Mark.) And further, in answer to the question of the disciples, "Why say the Scribes that Elias must first come?" Jesus "answered and told them, Elias verily cometh first and restoreth all things; and how it is written of the Son of Man, that he must suffer many things, and be set at nought." Here it is seen, that the theme upon which Jesus *began* to teach, just after Peter's noble confession, was speedily resumed again.

Yet only three of the Apostles witnessed the transfiguration, and heard the instruction given in connection with it. Soon after this, however, indeed the very next day, as appears from Luke's narrative,—Jesus teaches the same lesson, in explicit terms, to the whole company of the Twelve.*

Leaving the region of Cesarea Philippi, the scene of his transfiguration and of his healing the demoniac boy, and journeying into Galilee, he introduces the subject, in connection with his former miracle. The people had greatly wondered over that miracle. They seem to have uttered their admiration in unwonted applauses. And Jesus, amidst the echoes of these applauses, admonishes his disciples of his coming humiliation and death. He

* See Matt. xvii. 22, 23, and its parallels.

says, "Let these sayings sink down into your ears: for the Son of man shall be delivered into the hands of men." (Luke.) The time was at hand in which such tokens of his Almighty power as had recently been exhibited, might be forgotten in his seeming helplessness in the hands of his enemies. On the way to Galilee, and while sojourning in that country, Jesus remains in seclusion with his disciples, in order that he may speak with them yet more fully. And Matthew and Mark record the repeated prediction of his death and resurrection, and with Luke intimate the new circumstance of his betrayal to his enemies. "The Son of man shall be betrayed into the hands of men." Thus plainly did Christ *continue* the teaching which he before "began." The disciples very imperfectly understood the true meaning of his words; yet they understood enough to be greatly saddened. The subject was of such mysterious nature that they shrank from questioning the Saviour for any explanation of his meaning.*

Not long after this, Jesus having for a long time avoided Jerusalem, because of the deadly hostility of the Jews, secretly goes up to the city, and suddenly throws

---

* Remembering the familiarity of the disciples with the Master, it may at first seem to us strange that they should hesitate to speak with him freely upon this subject. In a comment of singular impressiveness, on Mark ix. 32, ALEXANDER observes, that the reticences which we are accustomed instinctively to practice towards one another, even when most familiarly acquainted and tenderly related, are equally difficult of rational explanation. The personality of every one is sacred. Nothing stands more closely related to our personality than death. There was that in the personality of Jesus, the eternal Son of God, yet the mortal Son of man, which was awfully mysterious. After the resurrection, Jesus appearing to his disciples on the shore of the sea of Galilee, "none of them durst ask him, who art thou, knowing that it was the Lord." (John xxi. 12.)

himself into the midst of his foes.* He begins that ministry in which he is confronted by the chiefs of the nation, eager for his destruction. With his life in his hand, he attacks Pharisaism in its stronghold, vindicates at the National Capital and in the presence of all people, his Divine Sonship and Messiahship, even as it behooved him to do, before he should die. On this occasion, he warns the people that he is to be with them only "a little while."† Having retired for a brief period into Perea, and going up thence to Jerusalem for the last time, he again, while on the way, takes his disciples aside, and admonishes them that the hour of his sufferings and death is at hand.‡

This further distinct announcement is of peculiar interest. It was made under a singular stress of feeling, on the part of both the Master and his disciples. Mark informs us that "they were in the way, going up to Jerusalem; and Jesus went before them: and they were amazed; and as they followed, they were afraid. And he took again the twelve, and began to tell them what things should happen unto him." The prediction is now more full than ever. There is an enumeration of the indignities which should be committed against him, and the statement is made that he shall not only be betrayed to the chiefs of his own nation, but that they in turn shall deliver him to the Gentiles, who shall inflict the indignities mentioned, and at last put him to death *by crucifixion*. (Matthew.) As before, he clearly foretells his resurrection on the third day. And again we are

---

* John vii. 10, 14. † John vii. 33.
‡ Matt. xx. 17-19, and its parallels.

informed by Luke that the disciples failed to comprehend the Saviour's meaning.

In Jerusalem again, and engaged in his last conflicts with his enemies, we find him at one time tasting the bitterness of the anticipation of "his hour,"—such an anticipation as on the night before he suffered had well nigh crushed him, and which here brought from him the exclamation, "Now is my soul troubled and what shall I say?"* Again he warns the people to walk in the light while they have the light, lest speedy darkness overtake them.† Soon after, he is in the midst of his disciples, eating the passover with them, as he had greatly desired to do before he should suffer; announcing that he shall be betrayed by one of their own number; instituting the memorial supper; predicting the smiting of the Shepherd and the scattering of the flock; giving his last counsels and offering his last intercessory prayer; all being speedily followed by the dread events of his agony, his arrest, his trial, and his crucifixion.

Does not this brief survey of our Lord's ministry subsequent to the time before us, taken in connection with the fact that prior to this time no explicit teachings of the sort adverted to were given, sufficiently illustrate and confirm the statement, that just now commenced a new era in his ministry, an era which distinctly contemplated his death? "From that time forth" began Jesus, both to show to his disciples his approaching passion, now but a few months distant, and also to anticipate and prepare for it, in a more direct way than before.

It may be observed, before dismissing this subject,

* John xii. 27.   † John xii. 35.

that conceiving of our Saviour as now passing from his general ministry of active and varied labors, to his ministry of suffering—to that ministry in which the things of his mysterious passion rose into colossal prominence, and cast their awful shadow over his life—the events immediately preceding and following the announcement of our Saviour before us, have a new meaning.

The event immediately preceding is that of the disciples' distinct and solemn avowal of their faith in the Messiahship of Jesus, in contrast with the varying opinions of the people concerning him. While some said that Jesus was John the Baptist, others that he was Elijah, others that he was Jeremiah, or some one of the other old prophets returned to life, the disciples, upon the challenge of the Master, declared their faith in him as none other than the Messiah. And, in the light of the foregoing considerations, our Saviour is herein seen preparing the minds of his disciples for the announcement of what will sorely try their faith. It is as if he had said, "You are fully convinced that I am the Messiah: well, I shall now tell you some things which will wholly contradict your notions concerning the Messiah, and I desire you to have the evidences of my Messiahship clearly before you, that this new teaching may not shake your faith."

The event immediately following is that of the Transfiguration. Jesus was for a time personally glorified in the presence of three of his disciples. Two of the most illustrious personages in Jewish history, Moses, the founder of the Hebrew Economy, and Elijah, its great restorer, were present in glorified form, talking with

Jesus. The sole subject of their conversation, so far as we are informed, was "his decease which he should accomplish at Jerusalem." And, in the light of the foregoing considerations, how must Peter and his companions on the mount have wondered, when they found that the subject of Jesus' recent instructions, so unwelcome to themselves, was of absorbing interest to these distinguished, heavenly guests. And how well adapted to correct their false views must have been the discovery here made, that the idea of a dying Messiah, which they had regarded as foreign to their Scriptures, was, in the estimation of the two great representatives of the Law and of the Prophets, the grand idea. And how well adapted to correct their erroneous conceptions of what constituted the proper glory of Christ, to find Jesus all intent upon his coming humiliation even unto death, at the very moment that he was all radiant with more than earthly regal splendor.

XIII.

The Transfiguration occurring at Night.

Luke ix. 28–36; ix. 37.

PERHAPS we most commonly think of the Transfiguration as having occurred in the daytime. The scene, no doubt, would have been inconceivably glorious, had it occurred even at noonday. The light of heaven, as at Paul's conversion, would have outshone the brightness of the sun. Yet, in all probability, the Transfiguration occurred at night. And so thinking of it, our conception of the brilliancy of the scene is enhanced, rather than diminished. The light of heaven is then brought into contrast with earthly darkness, rather than into comparison with earthly light. It might indeed be imagined that the appearance of the *cloud*, in the scene of the Transfiguration, would have been more impressive by daylight than in the darkness; yet this would not have been, unless the cloud itself had been dark, which we know was not the fact. It was "a *bright* cloud" which "overshadowed them." The voice of God came from this cloud. Symbolical of God's presence, it was luminous, like the Shekinah, which overhung the mercy-seat of the ark of the covenant. The cloud being thus of bright and burning appearance, *its* brilliancy, like that of the other parts of the sublime scene, would be enhanced, rather than diminished, by appearing in contrast with the darkness of night.*

Now that the night, rather than the day, witnessed this scene, we might infer from two suggestions offered by the narrative itself. The first is this; that, according to Luke's account—Luke being here, as often elsewhere, intent on our Saviour's devotional habits—Jesus went up to the mount of Transfiguration for the purpose of prayer, and was actually transfigured while engaged in prayer. Luke writes, "he took Peter and John and James, and went up into a mountain *to pray*. And *as he prayed*, the fashion of his countenance was altered, and his raiment was white and glistering." And the gospel narratives abundantly inform us that it was *at night* that Jesus was accustomed to seek the solitudes for devotional purposes.†

"Cold mountains and the midnight air
Witnessed the fervor of his prayer."

The other suggestion also comes from a statement peculiar to Luke's narrative; to wit, that when the Transfiguration occurred, the disciples were oppressed with sleep. They did not, as it seems from the language of our version, witness the *act* of transfiguration. The change had already passed upon the Saviour, and the heavenly visitants had arrived, when the disciples awoke. Possibly the flashings of celestial glory may have awak-

* OLSHAUSEN observes that the words "overshadowed them" are used in regard to the light-cloud, only in so far as it prevented the disciples from seeing. The most intense light is equivalent to darkness. Hence, in the language of Scripture, the expressions are used synonymously, God dwelleth in "light inaccessible," and in "darkness."

† Matt. xiv. 23, 24; Mark i. 35; Luke vi. 12.

ened them.* Luke writes, "But Peter and they that were with him were heavy with sleep, and when they were awake, they saw his glory, and the two that stood with him." Are we not reminded of that night which followed not long after this, in which these same three Apostles were the only companions of the Saviour, and in which, while he prayed, they fell asleep?†

Now, connecting with these suggestions which come from the narrative, the statement made by Luke following his account of the Transfiguration, to wit, "And it came to pass, that on *the next day*, when they were come down from the hill, much people met him," it seems well nigh certain that the Transfiguration occurred at night.

It may be worth a closing observation, that the fact that the Evangelist Luke affords all these intimations concerning the Transfiguration occurring at night, indicates that he regarded this circumstance with peculiar interest.

* ALFORD *in loco* gives as the proper meaning of the word translated "when they were awake," *having kept awake*, and seems to think that the disciples had not fallen asleep. Accepting the translation, the inference is not necessary; but granting both, the argument remains the same for its being night-time. Indeed, ALFORD argues that it was night-time, and presents to such an extent the very same line of remark found in this chapter, that our view might be thought to have been *adopted* from him, which is not the case.

† Matt. xxvi. 40–45.

XIV.

The Transfiguration Scene culminating in the Heavenly Voice.

Matt. xvii. 5–7; ii Peter i. 17, 18.

NOT only did the Transfiguration scene end with the coming of the bright cloud which betokened the Divine presence, and the issuing of the Divine voice out of its bosom, but this was the point of intensest interest to the disciples.

The whole vision of the glorified Jesus and his celestial attendants was extatic, evoking from the bewildered Peter, when it seemed about to end, the exclamation intended to stay its ending, "Lord, it is good for us to be here: and let us make three tabernacles; one for thee, and one for Moses, and one for Elias." Yet not so profoundly impressive was this sight, as was that which followed. This we may see by a comparison of the records.

Mark informs us that at the time when Peter felt constrained to speak, the disciples were "sore afraid." Yet impressed as they already were, a still deeper awe stole upon them, as they beheld the bright overshadowing cloud about to envelop them; for Luke writes, "they feared as they entered into the cloud."* Yet a

* Some interpret the expression " they feared as they entered the cloud," that the disciples feared, when Moses and Elias entered the cloud. This seems unnatural; and the reason assigned for it by ALFORD, to wit, that if the disciples had entered the cloud, the voice would not have been heard "out of the cloud," has little force.

still profounder fear oppressed them, when from the cloud now surrounding them, came the heavenly testimony, sounding on the listening ear of night, "This is my beloved Son, in whom I am well pleased, hear ye him;" for Matthew writes, that "when the disciples heard it, *they fell on their face,* and were sore afraid." Like John in Patmos, before the majestic apparition of the Son of Man, they fell on their faces as dead, being directly confronted with the glory of God. And from their prostration they did not recover, until Jesus came to their relief, reassuring them, much as he did John in Patmos, by his touch and his voice.

And, now, how admirably confirmatory of this account, in which the impression of awe is seen to be constantly deepening, until at last, with the coming of the Divine voice, it is absolutely overpowering, is the statement which Peter makes concerning the Transfiguration, many years after, when he is shortly to put off his earthly tabernacle.

Few are the personal reminiscences of their intercourse with the Saviour, given by the disciples in their epistolary writings. Yet Peter makes an emphatic appeal to this most memorable occurrence on the mount of Transfiguration. And, calling the scene to mind, be it observed that he dwells particularly, not on the glory which Christ received from his being transfigured in person, not on the honor done him by the attendance of Moses and Elias, but solely on the honor which God the Father gave him, in the voice out of the cloud. "For," says the venerable Apostle, speaking as if in vivid view of the scene, and in tones suggestive of remaining awe, "we have not followed cunningly devised fables, when we made known unto you the power and coming of our Lord Jesus Christ, but were eye-witnesses of his majesty. For he received from God the Father honor and glory, when there came *such a voice* to him from the excellent glory, This is my beloved Son in whom I am well pleased. And *this voice* which came from heaven we heard, when we were with him in the holy mount."

XV.

The Exclamation, "O Faithless and Perverse Generation!" as uttered soon after the Transfiguration.

Matt. xvii. 17; 2-9.

DURING the temporary absence of Jesus, on the mount of Transfiguration, with "the three disciples chosen of the twelve," events of great interest were occurring in connection with the remaining disciples.

A man had brought his demoniac son to these disciples, and they had made an ineffectual attempt to heal him. There were Scribes present who did not fail to embrace this opportunity for "questioning with the disciples." No doubt these Scribes took advantage of their failure, to contest their claim to power over evil spirits, and perhaps the like claim of their Master. The poor disciples, mortified by their failure and unable to account for it,[*] were evidently hard pressed, when the Master opportunely arrives. Soon he transfers the controversy from them to himself, and shows himself master of the situation.[†]

[*] Matt. xvii. 19, 20.

[†] "But as when some great captain, suddenly arriving upon a field of battle, where his subordinate lieutenants have well nigh lost the day, and brought all into a hopeless confusion, with his eye measures at once the necessities of the moment, and with no more than his presence causes the tide of victory to turn, and everything to right itself again, so was it now. The Lord arrests the advancing and victorious foe; he addresses himself to the Scribes, and saying, 'What question ye with them?' takes the baffled and

Before the Scribes could respond to his inquiry, "What question ye with them?" a man of the company cries out. It is the father of the demoniac, who introduces and describes the case of his child. As this cry of the man is in response to the challenge of Jesus to the Scribes, (Mark) the supposition is confirmed that the Scribes were questioning the disciples concerning their failure with this demoniac.

The father, prostrating himself before Jesus, (Matthew) entreats his pity, enforcing his plea with the consideration that this is his "only child." (Luke.) And the case of the child, as the father describes it, is indeed lamentable. He was an *epileptic*, as all the accounts show. He was also disordered in his organs of *speech* and of *hearing*. (Mark.) And, still further, he was mentally deranged. (Matthew.) Thus the evil demon, in taking possession of the child, had run the whole range of its being, occupying every organ of the body and ascending the throne of the intellect, and now was rioting at will over the whole domain. The father does not fail to state that the disciples had measured strength with the demon, and had been baffled in their attempts to eject him.

And now there is heard from the Saviour that strange, that almost passionate exclamation, which is the object of our special attention. Never before have we heard from him anything resembling it. All the writers who record the miracle wrought in connection with it, are careful to give it, using almost the self-same words. He

hard-pressed disciples under his own protection, implying by his words, 'If you have any question, henceforth it must be with me.'"—TRENCH on the Miracles.

cries, "O faithless and perverse generation, how long shall I be with you? how long shall I suffer you?"

What was it that brought from our Saviour this language? Endeavoring to answer this question, we may find much, in the very circumstances at the moment existing, seemingly adapted to provoke the exclamation. In view of the whole scene about him, exhibiting a most defective faith on the part of his disciples, utter unbelief and malignant hostility on the part of the scribes, and probably a capricious spirit of curious and blind wonder, ready to applaud or decry the Saviour in alternate voices, on the part of the people;—in view of this, the generation with whom he had so long labored to such little purpose, might well seem faithless and perverse, and he might well desire relief from the toils and the persecutions which characterized his ministry among them.

Yet frequently before and after this, the Saviour may be seen in circumstances apparently as trying, when he utters no such word.* May there not have been something peculiar in the present case, which we have not yet noted? We think there was, and that the sacred narrative affords us the opportunity of seeing it.

Only a short time before this, as we have already observed, Jesus had begun, more distinctly than ever, to anticipate and speak of his coming death.† Now the thought of his death was, no doubt, usually attended with the distinct anticipation of his heavenly exaltation.

---

* The exclamation in Luke xii. 50, "But I have a baptism to be baptized with, and how am I straitened till it be accomplished," is somewhat similar, expressing a holy eagerness to realize the triumphs of his death.

† Matt. xvi. 21.

"Ought not Christ to have suffered these things, and to enter into his glory?" "Who, for the joy that was set before him, endured the cross." "The hour is come that the Son of Man should be glorified." Thoughts of his coming glory, then, had recently been much in the mind of Jesus, prior to the occasion before us. Not only so, but the very night preceding, he had enjoyed an actual experience of heavenly glory on the mount of Transfiguration. Just now he was fresh from the scene of his communings with Moses and Elias, and from the reception of the high honor of his Father's testified approbation.

And can we but think that it was the contrast of his anticipations of heaven with his experience of earth, and, especially, the sudden contrast of his blessed taste of heavenly honor and joy with the bitterness of his life amidst the dishonors of men, that extorted the cry, not only, "O faithless and perverse generation," but, "how long shall I be with you, how long shall I suffer you?" As if he had said, "O when shall the time arrive, that, these toils and sufferings accomplished, the glory, as of the mount of Transfiguration, shall be mine to enjoy, without measure and without end?"

XVI.

The Contentions of the Disciples among themselves; as always connected with Christ's Teachings concerning His Death.

Mark ix. 33, 34; x. 35-45; Luke xxii. 24-27.

ALMOST every reader of the gospels has, at some time or other, observed with surprise, that a disgraceful strife among the disciples, as to who of them should be the greatest in the kingdom of heaven, arose in close connection with the distinct instruction of our Saviour, of momentous and absorbing concern, in reference to his coming sufferings and death. Just when we should have expected them to be all intent on *his terrible humiliation*, predicted to them confidentially and with great solemnity, they are only concerned for *their own selfish exaltation* one above another.

But perhaps it escapes the observation of most readers, that these occasions of contention among the disciples, which were three in number, *invariably* followed upon such teachings of our Saviour, and that these occasions were the *only* ones in which, after the first announcement, our Saviour explicitly predicted to the Twelve his coming humiliation. Yet such is the fact. *Whenever* he spoke freely, to the company of his Apostles, of his expected humiliation, they began at once to dispute with one another concerning their expected exaltation.

We have already reviewed these peculiar teachings

with relation to another subject.* Let us now glance at them in reference to this.

The first occasion occurred, when they came from Cesarea Philippi to Galilee, after the Transfiguration and the miracle of healing the demoniac boy.† It would seem that it was while they were making their way toward Capernaum that Jesus spoke to them plainly of his impending death. Arriving at Capernaum, (Matthew and Mark,) "and being in the house, he asked them, What was it that ye disputed among yourselves *by the way?* But they held their peace; for *by the way* they had disputed among themselves, who should be the greatest." (Mark.) Then, setting a child in the midst of them, he inculcates the lesson of Christian humility. Thus, in this instance, stand in close proximity the teaching of the Saviour and the peculiar conduct of the disciples, the latter evidently following the former.

On the second occasion, they are going up to Jerusalem, when Jesus propounds his solemn teaching.‡ And *the very next thing* of which we read, in Matthew and Mark, is the request of James and John—made for them, as appears from Matthew, by their mother—that they may "sit the one on his right hand and the other on his left in his kingdom," and the indignation of the other ten at the proceeding. No wonder that Jesus admonishes the ambitious brothers that they know not what they ask, and at once speaks of the cup and the baptism of sufferings appointed him. And again, and in very impressive language, he inculcates the lesson of humility.

On the third occasion, the time of his appointed suffer-

---

* Ch. XII. † Matt. xvii. 22, 23, and parallels.
‡ Matt. xx. 17–19, and parallels.

ings is at hand. It is only the night before the crucifixion. They are just sitting down at the passover table.* He gives them very express intimations of the near approach of his death. He declares, "With desire have I desired to eat this passover with you before I suffer." And again, as we read, "there was also a strife among them, which of them should be accounted the greatest." And now he not only inculcates the lesson of humility, in language very similar to that employed on the preceding occasion, but, as we shall see in a subsequent chapter, enforces the lesson by that most impressive proceeding, in which he takes a towel and basin and washes his disciples' feet.†

Now, can we think that this frequent and invariable sequence of such peculiar conduct upon such peculiar teaching, was wholly fortuitous? This were in the highest degree improbable. We are almost compelled to think that the one was the natural result of the other. And looking to ascertain, if we may, this fact, we are led into a more impressive, if not a wholly new view, of the significance of these portions of the history.

We must remember, then, that it was the settled conviction of the disciples, that their Master would establish a glorious earthly kingdom, and would himself reign upon the throne of David his father. Whatever else *might* be true, this to their minds *must* be true. Whatever was inconsistent with this belief must either be rejected, or must be modified into possible harmony with this. Christ might tell them of his suffering at the hands of men, of his rejection and crucifixion, yet this, in its obvious meaning, contradicting their settled convictions,

* Luke xxii. 14, 15, 24.   † John xiii. 1-20; Ch. XXVII.

went with them for little or nothing. They would not deny it, yet they supposed it must be understood in some hidden and figurative sense, which would permit them still to hold their old notions. It must nevertheless be true, that Jesus would yet cast off his lowly guise, and take to himself his kingly power, and realize his kingly character; and when he should sit on his magnificent throne, they would be honored above all other men as his chief ministers.

And, in the several teachings of Christ concerning what was awaiting him in Jerusalem, while they failed to perceive the true meaning of the Master's language, they saw in it enough to convince them that *a grand crisis of some sort was at hand*. And whatever else might occur to him in this crisis—whatever his strange language might mean, concerning his betrayal, his crucifixion, and his resurrection—they had the strongest confidence that in the crisis he would take his throne and begin his reign. He would at that time "restore again the kingdom unto Israel." And *just in this way*, Christ's teachings, even concerning his humiliation, would set them upon thoughts of the worldly honors which they should enjoy in connection with his government, and occasion disputings for pre-eminence in these.

As confirmatory of this view, we may observe that the pre-eminence which the disciples aspired after is constantly conceived of as existing "in the kingdom of heaven," or under the Messiah's reign. Thus, on the first three occasions of their disputing, the controversy does not relate to pre-eminence in general. They ask the question, "Who is the greatest *in the kingdom of heaven?*" And Jesus, setting the little child in the midst of them, teaches them that they must humble themselves as little children in order to "enter *the kingdom of heaven.*" (Matthew.) So it is the ambitious request of James and John, to sit, the one on his right hand and the other on his left, "*in his kingdom,*" (Matthew,) or "*in his glory.*" (Mark.)

And, as partially explaining the error of the disciples, in adhering to the idea of a glorious worldly kingdom for the Messiah, and of honorable positions for themselves in that kingdom, even in spite of the Saviour's explicit instructions concerning his sufferings, we may observe that our Saviour often spoke of his kingdom and his glory, in close connection with his teachings concerning his humiliation. Thus, after his first announcement of his coming sufferings, and his notification to his disciples of the necessity of their taking up the cross and following him, he adds, "For the Son of Man shall come in the glory of his Father, with his angels; and then shall he reward every man according to his works. Verily I say unto you, there be some standing here, which shall not taste of death, till they see the Son of Man coming in his kingdom."* So, just before the first of the three occasions when the disciples disputed with one another, Jesus had spoken of the illustrious rewards which they should receive as his faithful followers, giving them the following distinct and emphatic assurance, "Verily I say unto you, that ye which have followed me in the regeneration, when the Son of Man shall sit in the throne of his glory, ye also shall sit upon twelve thrones judging the twelve tribes of Israel."† And at the passover table, not only did he say, "With desire have I desired to eat this passover with you before I suffer," but also, "I will

* Matt. xvi. 27, 28, and parallels.   † Matt. xix. 27–30, and parallels.

not any more eat thereof, until it be fulfilled in the kingdom of God," and "I will not drink of the fruit of the vine until the kingdom of God shall come."*

We cannot, then, greatly wonder that the disciples failed to perceive the true meaning of Christ's predictions concerning his sufferings. And, failing to perceive the true meaning of these predictions, and seeing in them only the tokens of a great revolution at hand, we cannot greatly wonder that, with their previous views of a literal and worldly kingdom of God, they were, with each new prediction of the Saviour, stirred to stronger anticipations of the setting up of such a kingdom, and to ambitious desires for its expected honors.

It is not inconsistent with what has been said, to suppose that, in each case of the contentions of the disciples, there was something in the circumstances of the moment, as well as in the fact of Christ's recent teaching, which incited them to controversy. As, in the second case presented, the conduct of James and John provoked the indignation of the other disciples, so, in the case preceding it, there may have been a jealousy existing with the nine disciples, for the peculiar favor shown the three who were chosen to attend the Saviour on the mount of Transfiguration. Likewise, in the case following it, the dispute may have begun with claims for positions of honor at the passover table. His teaching occasioned their speculations on the glorious rewards coming, and the natural desire for a superior share of these was provoked to express itself by the jealousies existing at the time.

* Luke xxii. 16, 18, 28–30.

XVII.

Conduct of the Unbelieving Brethren of Jesus; as seen on Two Occasions.

John vii. 2–10; Mark iii. 20, 21, 31–35.

FOR eighteen months, as is commonly estimated, Jesus had avoided Jerusalem. This he had done, because "the Jews sought to kill him." Meanwhile he had been prosecuting his ministry in Galilee and the regions adjacent.

The feast of Tabernacles is now to be celebrated, yet, it would seem, Jesus shows no sign of leaving his present place. He is quietly remaining in Galilee, while all around him are intent on the festival and are setting out for Jerusalem. "His brethren" are about leaving, and they urge him to go likewise. And they would have him appear in Jerusalem, as they allege, in order that he may publicly exhibit himself. Galilee was but an obscure, outlying province; Jerusalem was the great national capital, and now gathered the people from far and from near. If he desired to make himself known to his countrymen, it was, as they argued, unreasonable still to avoid publicity. Rather he should court it. He should avail himself of the opportunity afforded by the feast, at once to procure the national recognition of his claims. The language of his brethren is, "Depart hence, and go into Judea, that thy disciples also may see the works that thou doest. For there is no man that doeth anything in secret, and he himself seeketh to be known openly. If thou do these things, show thyself unto the world." We are given, further, distinctly to understand that his brethren did not credit his claims to be a high messenger from God, and that their remonstrance with him at this time was prompted by their want of faith. The Evangelist adds, "*For*, neither did his brethren *believe on him*."

This remonstrance of the brethren of Jesus has been understood in a variety of senses, some of them contradictory of each other. One class of commentators regard it in its most obvious sense, as expressive of a sincere desire that Jesus should go to Jerusalem and "do his works in the temple, and before the priests and rulers; because if recognized there, he would be everywhere received." Another class regard it as ironical and scornful, as expressive of contemptuous skepticism, as taunting him with cowardice in not venturing himself in Jerusalem. Now, what is the proper sense of the language of the brethren of Jesus?

This passage has a peculiar interest for its bearing on that most perplexing question, whether the persons named as James and Simon and Judas, in the catalogues of the Twelve, were identical with the persons of the same name spoken of as our Lord's brethren.* It does not belong to our present purpose to discuss this question. Rather we would interpret the passage, without reference to it. And we would interpret the passage mainly in the light of the history, and especially in the light of the conduct of these same brethren as exhibited on a former occasion.

* Luke vi. 15, 16; Matt. xiii. 55.

His brethren, then, "did not believe on him." Without insisting now on the precise import of these words, we may give their general meaning, as made probable by the whole history, on this wise.—They held him in sincere esteem as a near relative who was wholly inoffensive, and in the highest degree pure and loving, but they discredited his claims to be a mighty prophet. Having grown up in his company, being thoroughly familiar with him in his earthly relations, they failed to recognize in him what was Divinely extraordinary. They verified the proverb, used by our Saviour, "A prophet is not without honor, but in his own country, and among his own kin, and in his own house." And therefore they did not attend upon his ministry. They remained at Nazareth, while he was abroad performing his wonderful works, and uttering his wonderful words. Now, supposing that their want of faith in him was of this sort, are we to believe that, on the occasion before us, they sought to force Jesus upon greater publicity; or is it more probable that they sought to withdraw him even from the publicity in which he already lived? The conduct of these brethren, as once before shown, may help in the answering of this question. And what was that conduct?

Jesus had fully entered on his Galilean ministry. He was journeying from place to place, attended by a great throng, working his mightiest miracles and everywhere proclaiming the word. "His friends" hear of it. The fame of his doings penetrates to Nazareth, where they seem to be remaining—in strange apathy and unbelief. They hear particularly of the excited multitudes who besiege him at every moment. What they hear rouses their latent suspicions, that his enthusiasm has now mounted to the height of positive insanity. And their thought is, that it is time for them to interfere and put a stop to his proceedings. The language of the record is, "And the multitude cometh together again, so that they could not so much as eat bread. And when his friends heard of it, they went out to lay hold on him: for they said, He is beside himself."* Thus setting out, they by-and-by reach the place where he is teaching, where the multitude is so vast and dense that they cannot get access to him. And now we are informed just who these "friends" are. The word is passed to him, "Behold thy mother, and *thy brethren* stand without, desiring to speak with thee."†

Here, then, is another glimpse of "his brethren." They are unbelieving; and what are they doing? Why they are seeking to *recall him from publicity*, and bring him to retirement.

This being the case, how can we think that farther on in his ministry, they, remaining in the same state of mind toward him—still unbelieving—should urge an opposite course upon him? How can we think that he being comparatively quiet in Galilee, they should really desire him to go to Jerusalem, and act the part of a professed prophet in the presence of the assembled nation? Does it not rather seem, that now, while he was comparatively quiet, they regarded it as a favorable time to approach him again, and to renew the attempt to disenchant him of his delusions concerning himself, and to dissuade him from further following his strange manner of life?

* Mark iii. 20, 21. † Mark iii. 32.

This interpretation, suggested by the history, admirably falls in with the language of the brethren, closing their remonstrance; "*If thou do these things,* show thyself to the world." How naturally does this form of expression suggest the alternative, that it would be wise for him *not* to "do these things!" How naturally does it suggest the thought that the exposure of himself in Jerusalem is proposed by his brethren, only as an argument to enforce the necessity of his quitting public life altogether!

This, then, is our view of the passage in question. The unbelieving brethren of Jesus, in their remonstrance with him, endeavored to show the inconsistency of his course in remaining away from Jerusalem, with his claim to be a prophet of God. And this they did, not with the desire of having him go to Jerusalem and there assert his claim, but with the hope of inducing him to renounce his assumed character altogether. They meant to persuade him that his very dread of appearing in Jerusalem was conclusive proof of his *not* being a mighty prophet.

We may regard their language as not that of scorn, but that of kind rebuke. It is as if they had said, "You profess to be sent of God, perhaps to be the Messiah himself. Yet you do not venture to submit your claims to a public test. You do not place yourself where you can realize your vocation. If yours is a Divine mission to your countrymen, you need to go before them, at the National Capital and, in the most public manner, vindicate and discharge that mission. This you refuse to do. You have assumed a character which you cannot maintain. Now our advice is, either to go up to Jerusalem at once, and make good your claim and perform your prophetic work; or, still unwilling to undertake this, to abandon these wild notions concerning yourself, and this strange manner of conduct, and come home to sober life."

E*

XVIII.

The Allegory of the Good Shepherd; as connected with the Healing of the Man born blind.

John ix.; x.

THE division of the sacred writings into chapters, while convenient for reference, is often unhappy in breaking up connections in thought. We can hardly help feeling that what has always been presented us, and has been read by us, in separate chapters, is disconnected in sense. Thus we sometimes miss the continuity of thought preserved in successive chapters, and fail to see the contents of one chapter in the light which its neighbor might throw upon it.

These observations apply emphatically to the division of John's gospel between the ninth and tenth chapters. The latter opens with the allegory of the Good Shepherd. And inasmuch as this begins a new chapter, many persons fail to perceive that it has any connection with what precedes. Yet the allegory was, in all probability, directly occasioned by the events detailed in the previous chapter, and is all the more forcible when viewed in their light. Let us see.

The ninth chapter is chiefly occupied with an account of the man blind from his birth, who was healed by Jesus. The Saviour was now in Jerusalem. The time is subsequent to the feast of tabernacles. From Galilee he has come suddenly, during the feast, into the midst of the gathered multitudes, and is now openly vindicating his high claims to Divine Sonship and Messiahship against the determined and fierce opposition of the chiefs of the nation. When he encounters the blind man, who is the prominent person in this chapter, he has just avoided being stoned by the Jews in the temple. No sooner is he out of their reach, than he begins his labors anew, saying, " I must work the works of him that sent me, while it is day : the night cometh, when no man can work."

All are familiar with the outline of narrative following; how Jesus, anointing the eyes of the man, sends him to wash in the pool of Siloam, which results in his cure; how the man's neighbors, disputing among themselves concerning his identity and his cure, bring him to the Pharisees; how these interrogate, first the man and then his parents, regarding the whole matter; how, when the Pharisees denounce Jesus, the man takes ground in favor of him, arguing his Divine mission; and how, at last, the incensed and scornful Pharisees pass upon the man the dread sentence of excommunication from the synagogue and banish him from their company as unclean and vile. And few stories of life, either inspired or uninspired, so stir our manly sympathies, as does this account of a poor beggar just emerging from life-long blindness, who, confronted with the magnates of the land singly and alone, deserted even by his own parents, harried with examinations and cross-examinations, and hearing his benefactor foully calumniated—the account of this man, in these circumstances, maintaining an unbroken, fearless, cheerful spirit, and, with blunt words of honest indignation, tearing in pieces the sophistries of his teachers, hurling back their vile imputations cast upon his benefactor—stoutly maintaining his Divine mission; thus, utterly regardless of personal consequences, exasperating them to fury.

Yet the condition of the man, now driven from the synagogue and from society, is indeed deplorable. What will become of him? Who will befriend him? Faithful, where so many are faithless, shall he have no reward? A true sheep of the flock of Israel, shall he be left to wander, unsheltered and unguided, amidst the wilds upon which he is cast? Not so. A friend is at hand. A good Shepherd is near.

At the time of his working this miracle, Jesus was retreating from his enemies for safety. And for a while he remains aloof. But when he hears that the man has been cast out, he goes in quest of him, at all hazards. All along, no doubt, he had well known what was going on, and was in lively sympathy with his new disciple, so nobly confessing him. "Perhaps in secret he was uttering, 'with strong crying and tears,' the words of the prophetic psalm, 'Let not them that wait on thee, O Lord God of hosts, be ashamed for my sake; let none that seek thee be confounded for my sake, O God of Israel: because for thy sake I have borne reproach, . . . and the reproaches of them that reproached thee are fallen upon me.'"* And in the young man "were to be fulfilled in a very eminent sense those words, 'Blessed are ye when men shall hate you, and when they shall separate you from their company, and shall reproach you, and cast out your name as evil for the Son of Man's sake.' He

* Prof. Brown's Notes on the Gospels.

is cast out of the meaner fellowship, to be received into a higher. 'When my father and my mother forsake me, the Lord will take me up.'"* "Man's extremity is God's opportunity," and at the darkest moment of the man's trial, Jesus comes upon him, reveals himself as his benefactor and the Son of God, and takes the outcast to fellowship with himself.

Now it is in close connection with this whole proceeding, a proceeding which in the strongest manner exhibits both the Jewish Rulers, as exerting their authority to the destruction of God's true people, and the Lord Jesus, as acting the part of a Saviour and Comforter to such, that Jesus utters his famous allegory, in which he proclaims himself the Good Shepherd, and characterizes those who have preceded him, as hirelings, thieves, and robbers. And does not this whole representation become emphatic, in view of the foregoing proceeding? How true, as seen in the case of the blind man and the Saviour, that the "sheep hear his voice," and that "he calleth his own sheep by name and leadeth them out." How true, as seen in the conduct of the Rulers toward the blind man, that "the thief cometh not, but for to steal, and to kill, and to destroy."

* Trench on the Miracles.

XIX.

The Request, "Lord, suffer me first to go and bury my Father;" by whom made, and why refused.

Matt. viii. 21, 22; Luke ix. 59, 60.

PROFESSOR BLUNT, in his "Undesigned Coincidences," from a comparison of passages in Matthew's gospel, infers that this request came from one of the sons of Zebedee. The request was certainly made by one "of his *disciples;*" for this is expressly stated; but whether the word "disciples" is here to be taken in the strict sense of Apostles, or the wider sense of the Seventy, or in the still more general sense of all believers, we must judge from the circumstances.

Prof. Blunt argues that this disciple was one of the sons of Zebedee, from the fact that *before* this Zebedee is mentioned as living—James and John, at the time of their call to the Apostleship, being spoken of as "in a ship with Zebedee their father;" while *after* this, the narrative implies that Zebedee was dead—the mother of James and John being spoken of, not as the wife of Zebedee, but as "the mother of Zebedee's children."*

Almost fearing, lest he should subject himself to the charge of over-refinement, the Professor ventures to infer "that the death of Zebedee is here alluded to, [that is, in the above request,] and that St. Matthew, without a

---

* Compare Matt. iv. 21; xx. 20; xxvii. 56.

wish, perhaps, or thought, either to conceal or express the individual, (for there seems no assignable motive for his studying to do either,) betrays an event familiar to his own mind, in that inadvertent and unobtrusive manner in which the truth so often comes out."

Our Saviour's refusal of the disciple's request, and the peculiar language in which it was couched, "let the dead bury their dead," have occasioned commentators much difficulty. Under ordinary circumstances such a request would seem perfectly proper. It would be made, indeed, as the dictate of filial piety. Why, then, was it now refused? A recent judicious expositor writes thus; "The reply of our Lord to the young man's request seems harsh, but he must have had special reasons for answering thus unknown to us."* A further study of this passage, in its various relations, elicits, we think, a confirmation of Blunt's view just given, and at the same time helps us in the conjecture of those "special reasons" which dictated the Saviour's reply.

Turning to the parallel passage in Luke, we find that while it is not there stated that the request came from one "of the disciples," the reply of our Saviour indicates that it *did* come from one who was formally and officially attached to his ministry. The reply is, "Let the dead bury their dead, *but go thou and preach the kingdom.*" The person was evidently an ordained ambassador of Christ. Further, that the disciple was one of the Twelve, rather than one of the Seventy, seems probable, from the fact that, at the time the request was made, the Seventy had not yet been commissioned.† Still further, that the

* Rev. Dr. Nast. Commentary on Matthew and Mark.
† Luke x. 1.

disciple was one of the sons of Zebedee, is suggested by the fact that James and John are mentioned by Luke in close connection with the request, and at a time when, as it appears, the Twelve had been sent out to prepare the way for our Saviour's progress toward Jerusalem. James and John seem to have been the two disciples who encountered the ill reception at the hands of the Samaritans, going thence to make report to their Master, and proposing to call down fire from heaven as Elias did. They were probably alone with the Master at the time, the rest of the Twelve being absent upon the important work recently assigned them. Close upon this incident comes the request under discussion, as though offered by one of these disciples.

Yet the inquiry is still more interesting, why did the Saviour refuse the request? What were his "special reasons?" If we may suppose that Luke, rather than Matthew, records this incident in its true chronological order, we may find the answer to this inquiry *in the peculiar circumstances of the Saviour and of his disciples at the time the request was made.*

* There is no good reason for *not* regarding this incident as recorded in its proper place by Luke. Matthew gives it as if occurring at a much earlier period of our Lord's ministry; recording it, as Luke also does, in connection with the incident of the man saying to Christ, "I will follow thee whithersoever thou goest," to whom the Saviour responds, "The foxes have holes, and the birds of the air have nests, but the Son of Man hath not where to lay his head." Luke gives, also, a third similar incident, omitted by Matthew. The Harmonists have been much perplexed in choosing between the Evangelists, and some of them have gone so far as to suppose that the very same incidents occurred *twice*, at the times severally mentioned by the two writers.

Our view is this: The order, as given by *each* of the writers is the order of actual occurrence, so far as *some one of the incidents* is concerned. Probably the interview with Jesus of "the Scribe," to whom Jesus declared,

THE UNSEASONABLE REQUEST.

Just now, our Saviour was about starting from Galilee to Jerusalem. On the way, he intended to employ himself in such thorough labors as he had already performed in Galilee, where he "went about all" the country, "teaching in their synagogues, and preaching the gospel of the kingdom, and healing all manner of sickness." To facilitate his plan, he made use of his Apostles as heralds, sending them out along the whole front of his advance, preaching the kingdom of God. Shortly before the incident in question is narrated, we have the following statement; "And it came to pass, when the time was come that he should be received up, he steadfastly set his face to go up to Jerusalem, and sent messengers before his face."* These messengers, who were probably the Apostles only, were not, it appears, sufficient for the whole work of making ready for him, which he now desired to have performed. For we read presently, that "after these things, the Lord appointed other Seventy also, and sent them two and two before his face, into every city and place, whither he himself would come."† Indeed, even this number was found to be painfully inadequate to the required work; for our Lord immediately after

---

"The foxes have holes," etc., occurred at the time indicated by Matthew, when Jesus was about to embark for the farther side of the lake. And probably the similar incidents, first, of the disciple who desired to go and bury his father, and secondly, of another who wished to go and bid farewell to his friends at home, occurred at the time indicated by Luke. It would be altogether natural for an Evangelist, in recording an incident occurring at a specified time, to associate with it a similar incident occurring at a different time.

It may be added that Prof. Blunt's argument, as stated above, is not impaired by the supposition that Luke, rather than Matthew, has recorded the incident in question in its true chronological order.

* Luke ix. 51, 52.   † x. 1.

thus speaks; "The harvest truly is great, but the laborers are few; pray ye therefore the Lord of the harvest, that he would send forth laborers into his harvest."* And that his disciples were to "preach the kingdom of God," we learn from the commission given to the Seventy; the only thing which they were specifically commanded to say being this, "The kingdom of God is come nigh unto you."†

Such, then, were the *circumstances* under which one "of the disciples" made the request that he might be permitted to go and bury his father. Whether or not this disciple was one of the Twelve, being one who had accepted the commission to "preach the kingdom of God," and offering his request at the precise time that there was an urgent and indispensable need for this preaching, "the special reasons" of the Master for refusing what, in the case of another, or in the case of this person at another time, might have been granted, seem sufficiently disclosed. Just now, it would be a forsaking of the service of Christ, for one of his disciples to leave him on such an errand. Just here, a test of the disciple's *paramount* devotion was reached. Jesus' words must

---

* Luke x. 2.

† Luke x. 9. We follow Robinson's Harmony whenever practicable. In this part of the history, we have felt compelled to deviate from it. We would place our Lord's final departure from Galilee and the sending out of the Seventy, subsequent to the feast of tabernacles. (John vii. 2.) For an admirable discussion of the chronology here, see "The Life of our Lord upon the Earth; considered in its Historical, Chronological, and Geographical Relations," by Samuel J. Andrews. Mr. Andrews very justly remarks, after a discussion concerning our Lord's last journey to Jerusalem, that if the character of this journey "be correctly stated, it is apparent that to the mission of the Seventy a much greater importance must be given than has usually been done by Commentators and Harmonists."

now receive their illustration, "He that loveth father or mother *more than me*, is not worthy of me."

And well might the disciple commit even the burying of his father to such as had assumed no obligations which would interfere with the performance of that work. Those who sustained no living relations to the kingdom of God—those "dead"—might be left to "bury their dead."

XX.

Christ Beholding the Young Ruler; as illustrated by His turning and looking on Peter.

Mark x. 21; Luke xxii. 61.

THE first three Evangelists narrate the incident of Christ's interview with the young Ruler. Each writer mentions certain particulars omitted by the others. The circumstance referred to in the title of this chapter, is given by Mark alone. In the midst of his narrative, Mark writes, "Then Jesus beholding him loved him."

In order that this circumstance may appear in full relief, let us review the accounts of the writers up to the point at which it is introduced, with some endeavor to understand the meaning of our Saviour's procedure as therein set forth.

Matthew, at the outset, is very indefinite; "And behold, one came and said unto him." Mark tells us where Jesus was. He has informed us before of Jesus being "in the house," where he had blessed the little children.* Now "he was gone forth into the way," probably having resumed his journey toward Jerusalem.

The action of the person approaching the Saviour, is also described by Mark. "There came one running and kneeled to him." Luke informs us that this person wa. "a certain *ruler*," one occupying an important ecclesiastical

* Vs. 10, 13.

position, and it falls out afterward, in Matthew's account, that he was a "*young* man."

His great question and its answer receive substantially the same record, in all the accounts. Addressing the Saviour as "Good Master," he asks what he shall do that he may inherit eternal life. Jesus, after an intimation that the young man's conceptions of spiritual excellence are superficial and unworthy, answers his question by referring him to the law. "And Jesus said unto him, why callest thou me good? There is none good but one, that is God. Thou knowest the commandments: Do not commit adultery, Do not kill, Do not steal, Do not bear false witness, Defraud not, Honor thy father and mother." (Mark.) Only Matthew records the question of the ruler, "which" of the commandments? in response to which the preceding enumeration is given; Matthew adding, "and thou shalt love thy neighbor as thyself."

The Master sends the ruler to the law, not to leave him there, but to lead him thence. Jesus will first discover to the ruler his self-righteous spirit, and then bring him to see and feel that the law, instead of affording any encouragement to such a spirit, on the contrary convicts of sin and argues the need of a Saviour.

The question of the young man, "which" of the commandments, shows that he regarded obedience to the law, as a formal compliance of conduct with the letter of the several precepts, rather than a conformity of heart to the principles underlying all the precepts.

Jesus enumerates the commandments of the Second table of the law, rather than the First, we may suppose, either because these afforded the easier test of character, or because the ruler's attention had all along been chiefly directed to these, and he had come to pride himself on his unexceptionable performance of social duties.

And now is brought from him that confession of his self-righteous confidence and hope, which, doubtless, the Saviour from the first intended to elicit, a confession made, as we have every reason to think, in all sincerity and with no little self-gratulation, "All these have I kept from my youth up." Having recognized in the Galilean teacher, one who had great discernment and skill in religious things, the young ruler had evidently come to him for a confirmation of present hopes, rather than for any new light concerning the way of life. He has now apparently received his desire, and having declared his faithful observance of the law, he sounds the challenge as of triumph, "What lack I yet?" This is recorded by Matthew alone, yet is implied by both the others.

Thus has the young man declared his whole heart. He stands before the Saviour fully revealed. It is a time of intense interest. The Master's soul has been kindling with all pure and pitying affections, in proportion as the false hopes of the ruler have been gaining strength and encouragement.* In faithfulness Jesus must now sorely

---

* The intense interest with which the Saviour entered into the case of the ruler, is further evident from the energetic expressions which he uses when the ruler withdraws. As if viewing with profound sorrow and indignation the ruinous influence of a love of wealth, he utters one astounding exclamation after another—"How hardly shall they that have riches enter into the kingdom of God!" "It is easier for a camel to go through the eye of a needle, than for a rich man to enter into the kingdom of God!" "With men this is impossible."

Some of the Commentators regard the question, "What lack I yet?" as indicative of the feeling of uneasiness and doubt, on the part of the ruler, and of a sincere desire to be more fully instructed in the way of life.

disappoint and grieve his questioner. He must dissipate his cherished self-deceptions. He must, with a single breath, blow upon his life-long hopes, and blast them forever. He will open the true way to eternal life, but how narrow is that way—how self-denying—perhaps too much so for the disappointed one to be willing to enter it.

We might have inferred that at this point Jesus would be deliberate in his utterances. We might have known that he would not rudely or violently tear away from the young ruler even the unworthy hopes with which he had deluded himself. And this, which we might have inferred, is distinctly intimated by the Evangelist Mark.

Nay more, not only was there a solemn pause in the conversation, not only did the eager question, "What lack I yet?" remain for a moment unanswered, but that moment was occupied by the Saviour in a most significant manner. *He turned himself in full upon the young man and earnestly surveyed him;* " *Then* Jesus *beholding* him."

And here it is that we would adduce the passage from the history of Peter's denials of his Master. Would we know how unutterably and thrillingly significant was *the look of Jesus*, we may judge of it from the case of Peter.* What volumes of pity and reproach must have been spoken, when "the Lord turned, and looked upon Peter," to have instantly brought the disciple to full recollection, and flooded his heart with penitent griefs, and

---

(LANGE, STIER, NAST, and others.) This, we think, does not so well accord with his subsequent conduct, in which he rejects the Saviour's prescription.

* The word "beholding," in Mark x. 21, is, in the Greek, a participle of the *same verb* translated "looked," in Luke xxii. 61.

sent him forth into the lonely night with tears of bitter weeping. And although the look of Jesus, in the case of the young ruler, may not have had precisely the same, yet it doubtless had an equal significance. And as we know, from the conduct of Peter, what was the peculiar meaning of the Saviour's look in his case, so we know, from the record itself, what was the peculiar meaning of the look which Jesus gave the young ruler. For Mark writes, "Then Jesus beholding him *loved him.*" The volumes now spoken were of pity and compassion. The soul of Jesus yearned upon this young man, so sincere, so upright, so deferential to himself, so concerned for his eternal prospects, yet so fatally mistaken. In that look perhaps, the young man, stirred with strange and profound emotions, read the coming answer of the Master. So did it penetrate and subdue his soul, that when the answer came, he had no disposition to question or resist its truth. He silently submitted to the terrible loss of all his hopes of heaven, being still more deeply attached to his great worldly possessions.*

Jesus' answer is, "One thing thou lackest," bidding him distribute his goods to the poor, and engage in the self-denying life of a disciple. Matthew writes, "If thou wilt be perfect, go and sell that thou hast, and give

---

* "The Spirit who accompanied the words of Jesus had deeply penetrated his heart, had enlightened the darkness within, had revealed to him the true, though hitherto entirely unknown, way of regeneration, and so he found himself taken prisoner by the power of the truth. But the chain which he carried was too heavy, he could not call forth within his heart that free determinate choice in favor of the narrow way, which is absolutely necessary, and the scarcely opened gate of Paradise closed itself again before his weeping eyes."—OLSHAUSEN, on Matt. xix. 22.

to the poor, and thou shalt have treasure in heaven: and come, follow me."

The ruler lacked *one* thing, but that was vital to everything else. It was not one thing of the same sort with the many things which he already possessed, needed simply to give completeness to his character. It was not a unit which must be added to the ninety-nine before possessed, to make a perfect hundred. It was not a little finger, as has sometimes been said, which was wanting, in order to a perfect physical man. Rather, the ruler needed a *principle* to animate his works of righteousness. He was destitute of that true love to God which is the life of all obedience to his law. The one thing which he lacked was the numeral 1, which preceding the ciphers, 00, worthless in themselves, *makes* them 100. It was not a little finger, needed to complete the man, but a *soul* to give life to the body. His heart was supremely set on worldly wealth. This was the idol on the throne. And therefore the Saviour enjoins upon him just that which would sacrifice the idol and enthrone the Lord in its stead.

The language of the Evangelists shows his failure to abide the Master's test, and at the same time his conviction of his life-long error. He is "sorrowful," (Matthew,) "very sorrowful," (Luke,) "sad" and "grieved." (Mark.) And going away, clinging to his "great possessions," he calls from the Master the exclamation, "How hardly shall they that have riches enter into the kingdom of God."

XXI.

Parable of the Laborers in the Vineyard; as connected with previous Teachings.

Matt. xx. 1–16; xix. 16–30.

THE disposition to sever parables from the connection in which they are found, and having isolated them to try and discover in their every feature and detail a resemblance to some supposed case—this disposition, more than anything else, as we believe, hinders the proper understanding of the parables. Such a disposition freely indulged, in reference to those incidents and anecdotes which, in modern discourse, are most nearly analogous to the parables of Scripture, would certainly be fatal to any correct understanding of them.

The parable of the laborers runs thus: "For the kingdom of heaven is like unto a man that is an householder, which went out early in the morning to hire laborers into his vineyard. And when he had agreed with the laborers for a penny a day, he sent them into his vineyard. And he went out about the third hour, and saw others standing idle in the market-place, and said unto them, Go ye also into the vineyard; and whatsoever is right, I will give you. And they went their way. Again he went out about the sixth and ninth hour, and did likewise. And about the eleventh hour he went out, and found others standing idle, and saith unto them, Why stand ye here all the day idle? They say unto him, Because no man hath hired us. He saith unto them, Go ye also into the vineyard; and whatsoever is right, that shall ye receive. So when even was come, the lord of the vineyard saith unto his steward, Call the laborers and give them their hire, beginning from the last unto the first. And when they came that were hired about the eleventh hour, they received every man a penny. But when the first came, they supposed that they should have received more; and they received likewise every man a penny. And when they had received it, they murmured against the good-man of the house, saying, These last have wrought but one hour, and thou hast made them equal unto us, which have borne the burden and heat of the day. But he answered one of them, and said, Friend, I do thee no wrong: didst not thou agree with me for a penny? Take that thine is, and go thy way: I will give unto this last, even as unto thee. Is it not lawful for me to do what I will with mine own? Is thine eye evil because I am good? So the last shall be first, and the first last: for many be called, but few chosen."

This is said to be one of the most difficult of the parables. And viewed apart from its connection, and regarded less for its governing thought than for the supposed significance of its several features, we may readily become bewildered in a maze of interpretations suggested by the imagination. And we are the more likely to view this parable apart from the previous context, with which it is vitally connected, for the reason that it is separated from that context in the artificial division of the chapters. The remarks made on p. 106 apply here with full force.

Very many readers, no doubt, have the impression that the twentieth chapter of Matthew opens with a wholly new subject.

We desire now, if possible, to obliterate this false impression. We desire to bridge the chasm which is produced by the division of the chapters, and draw the parable to its proper place, in immediate and living connection with our Lord's previous teaching. And we would seek to understand the parable in the light of that teaching. For this is one of the instances, in which a view of the whole is most important in order to a right understanding of the parts. Here, as often elsewhere, the motion of the river's current previously acquired may bear the vessel over a shallow passage of the stream, with only slight hindrance, when without such motion the vessel would have hopelessly grounded.*

That the parable was meant to illustrate and enforce the previous teaching, is evident from two considerations. First, the parable opens in a way to indicate it. The language is, "*For* the kingdom of heaven is like unto a man," etc. Plainly thus are we advertised of the connection of the parable with what goes before. In the second place, the parable winds up with a distinct reference to the saying of our Saviour immediately preceding, and with its partial repetition. The closing words of the nineteenth of Matthew are these; "But many that are

---

* NEANDER has some strange remarks on this point. He says, "We cannot but suppose that this parable is joined to the words that precede and follow by a merely accidental link of connection. The most elaborate efforts to harmonize the passages in question with the parable only result in destroying its sense, so pregnant with characteristic Christian truth." Yet he adds, "The collocation of the parable in Matthew may afford a clue to its interpretation."—LIFE OF CHRIST.

first shall be last; and the last first." And the parable thus concludes; "So the last shall be first and the first last; for many be called, but few chosen."

Instead, then, of looking at the parable separately, and spending our time in conjectures as to who respectively are represented by the laborers employed early in the morning, and at the different times of day mentioned; instead of trying to reconcile the dissatisfied and selfish spirit exhibited by those who had labored the whole day with what we know to be the true Christian spirit; instead of seeking to explain the equality of rewards in the parable consistently with the inequality of rewards which the Scriptures teach us to expect in heaven; instead of this, let us look at the great teaching of the previous context which the parable was evidently intended to re-exhibit and reinforce, and see if, in the view of the central and controlling truths of that teaching, the parable may not show an intelligible and impressive harmony.*

Our Saviour's previous teaching had been given in answer to a statement and inquiry made by the Apostle

* The Commentators are especially perplexed over the "penny." About one-half of them interpret it of *temporal* rewards; about one-half of *eternal*. A difference truly. But why should we interpret it of either? Why should we make puzzles of parables? Were not the parables intended as *illustrations* of truth? How then can they be regarded as *in themselves obscure?*

"The meaning of the denary (the penny) is a *crux interpretum*, and reminds us of what Chrysostom and Maldonatus say *in loc.*, that we must not scrupulously press every particular in a parable, but keep always in view the general scope. Parables are poetic pictures taken from real life for the illustration of the higher truths and realities of the kingdom of heaven, and contain with the essential figures some ornamental touches which are necessary for the artistic finish, although they may not express definitely a corresponding idea or fact in the spiritual world."—SCHAFF in LANGE, *in loco.*

Peter. "Then answered Peter, and said unto him, Behold, we have forsaken all, and followed thee; what shall we have therefore?" Now this question concerning the rewards of discipleship was not, in itself considered, unworthy. The disciple is expected to have some "respect unto the recompense of the reward." Our Saviour, therefore, does not refuse to answer Peter, but on the contrary portrays in most striking language the compensations of a true Christian self-denial. "And Jesus said unto them, Verily I say unto you, That ye which have followed me in the regeneration, when the Son of Man shall sit in the throne of his glory, ye also shall sit upon twelve thrones, judging the twelve tribes of Israel. And every one that hath forsaken houses, or brethren, or sisters, or father, or mother, or wife, or children, or lands, for my name's sake, shall receive an hundred fold, and shall inherit everlasting life."

Still, it would be easy to ask the question of Peter in an improper spirit. There was danger that with such inspiring rewards in prospect, some persons might undertake the Christian life simply with a view to secure them—in a selfish and mercenary spirit, rather than in the loving spirit of a true disciple. This were a fatal error. And hence the caution with which the Saviour follows his statements of the Christian's glorious rewards; "But many that are first shall be last; and the last first." The reward does not so much depend upon the *amount* of sacrifice made, or service rendered, as upon the prompting motive of the disciple. If the Christian serves his Master selfishly, less from love than he ought, and with an undue regard for advantage, though he be first in the matter of privations and toils, he shall be last in the matter of reward; while he who is truly devoted to the Master, being sacrificed in spirit, and ready lovingly to endure and labor according to his opportunities,—he, even though few opportunities be afforded him, and he be last in actual self-denials, shall be first in the matter of reward.

Next comes the parable. And regarding it as intended to enforce the caution just announced,—regarding it as intended to impress upon the Christian disciple the danger of indulging a selfish, hireling spirit when encouraging himself with the hope of reward,—how perfectly natural does it appear, how beautifully simple, how free from all that is perplexing. The Lord may do as he will with his own. His bestowments are of grace not of debt. Something else than the comparative amount of service rendered proportions the Christian's reward. The enjoyment of high Christian privilege, exciting selfish hopes but failing to secure the consecration of the heart to God, shall distinguish many who will come short of salvation. "So the last shall be first, and the first last: for many be called but few chosen."

XXII.

Christ's Triumphal Entry into Jerusalem: The Ass and her Colt.

Matt. xxi. 2, 7; Mark xi. 2; Luke xix. 30.

OUR Saviour coming up to Jerusalem for the last time before he suffers, enters the city as a king, amidst the acclamations of his loyal people. He does this, we may believe, not merely in order that the Scriptures may be fulfilled, but under the guidance of that eternal and infinite wisdom, which dictated both the prophecies of Scripture concerning him and the whole course of his actual life. It was doubtless needed that an open avowal of his Messiahship, of this impressive yet implicit sort, should be made at the Sacred Capital and in the presence of the Nation, before he should suffer. Gradually he had unfolded his character as the Messiah, and by implication had claimed to be recognized as such; and here the avowal is made so distinctly, that all pretence, on the part of those who should reject him, of his not claiming to be the Messiah, would be of no avail.

In the account given by the different Evangelists of the steps taken preliminary to the public entrance into the city, occurs a coincidence evidently unintended, but such as indicates the strict accuracy of each Evangelist, in narrating what was of special interest to himself or what was most suitable for his specific purpose

Mark and Luke speak of only *one* animal, in connection with Christ's riding into Jerusalem, and that "a colt." It was, too, an *unbroken* colt; for both writers are particular to state that never yet had man sat on it. This was doubtless a befitting circumstance in the arrangement. The present sacred service could not have been becomingly performed by an animal used before to common labors.

Turning now to Matthew, we find that he constantly speaks of *two* animals. "Ye shall find an ass tied, and a colt with her: loose them and bring them unto me." And it is only from the other Evangelists that we know upon which of the animals the Saviour rode, Matthew leaving this point undetermined.

On other occasions, as is well known, Matthew in like manner speaks of two objects or persons, where the other writers mention but one. Thus, "Coming into the country of the Gergesenes, there met him *two* possessed with devils."* The others speak of but one, whom we are accustomed from their narratives to call *the* Gadarene demoniac. So Matthew records the healing of two blind men at Jericho, where the others speak only of Bartimeus.† This peculiarity in Matthew is ascribed by some to his former practice of accurately noting numbers, in his occupation of accountant.

But while Matthew thus mentions the fact that the mother was taken along with the colt, without intimating any reason for it, the statement of the other writers, to the effect that the colt was unbroken and hence unaccustomed to being separated from its mother, furnishes us, although most incidentally, with a very obvious rea-

* Matt. viii. 28. † Matt. xx. 30.

son. The colt separated from its mother would have been intractable; especially when called to play an important part in a novel and exciting scene. The mother being led beside the colt, as Matthew's narrative implies that it was, no difficulty on this score would probably occur.

Thus the narratives, in a striking yet evidently undesigned manner, supplement each other.

If it be thought that we are refining unduly, it may be answered that it is no unimportant matter to detect an indication of accurate veracity on the part of the Evangelists, however nice; and that the nicer the indication the more important it is, for the purpose of showing their *infallible* truthfulness. And further, the refinement in this case is not without a sufficient result; inasmuch as it enables us to dispense with the supposition of a miracle performed on the colt, to make it sufficiently manageable. Many Commentators have thought the supposition of such a miracle necessary, although the records give no hint that any miracle was actually wrought.

We may add, before concluding, that the way in which Matthew speaks of the two animals, has curiously led him to the apparent assertion of a more *literal* fulfillment of prophecy than he evidently intended. Matthew thus writes; "And they brought the ass and the colt, and put on them their clothes, and they set him thereon." And before this he writes;* "All this was done, that it might be fulfilled which was spoken by the prophet, saying, Tell ye the daughter of Zion, Behold thy King cometh unto thee, meek, and sitting upon an

* Matt. xxi. 7.

ass, and a colt, the foal of an ass."* At first sight, we might have thought that the prophet had represented the King of Zion as riding on *two* animals, and that Matthew had spoken of both the ass and her colt, with a view of showing the exact fulfillment of the prediction. But every Hebrew scholar knows that only *one* animal was intended by the prophet; and it were absurd to think that Matthew, himself a Hebrew, would make a mistake here. Surely he was as familiar with the *parallelism* of Hebrew poetry, as are any of our modern critics!

* Matt. xxi. 4, 5.

XXIII.

The Miracle and the Parable of the Barren Fig-Tree.

Mark xi. 12-14; Luke xiii. 6-9.

OUR Saviour wrought many miracles of mercy in illustration of his gospel of mercy, but only one miracle of judgment in illustration of the wrath due to despised mercy. Even in this he selected an unconscious object for malediction and destruction.

The miracle of the barren fig-tree thus occurred. Jesus was at Jerusalem, teaching daily in the temple and spending his nights on the Mount of Olives. The people all came to the temple early in the mornings, thronging to hear him,* and he, working while the day lasted—his night hastening apace—came early into the city that he might be about his Father's business.

It was the next morning after his public entry into Jerusalem, that, returning from his night lodgings at Bethany, apparently without having breakfasted, he felt keenly the pangs of hunger. Seeing in the way a fig-tree in full leaf, he came to it, "if haply he might find anything thereon" to appease his hunger. But while there was an abundance of leaves, giving evidence of vigorous life, and, even in advance of the season, rich promise of fruit, no fruit was found. It was a barren fig-tree. In a few words, not of impatience or anger,

* Luke xxi. 38.

though doubtless of deep solemnity, he doomed the tree to the perpetual barrenness of death. "Jesus answered and said unto it, No man eat fruit of thee hereafter forever." And soon the judgment took effect. The next morning, that tree, so exuberant of a profitless life, flourishing in its showy, boastful wealth of leaves, was a withered mass, a lifeless stock, "dried up from the roots."

Now how is this miracle to be regarded? No doubt we might so conceive of it, that it would seem unworthy the Saviour.

We might conceive of it as exhibiting an ebullition of puerile resentment against an unconscious object which had innocently occasioned a disappointment. Of course there have not been found wanting those who were ready to make the most out of the apparently unfavorable features of this miracle.

Were it permitted us, however, to regard this miracle as mainly intended to teach important truth, all difficulty of the sort suggested would instantly vanish. And, as is well known, most interpreters attribute to it a symbolic character. They regard it as *a parable in action*, and as emblematical of the fate of the Jewish people. And that our Saviour intended the miracle thus to be taken, seems highly probable from the fact that just now the thought of the nation's approaching destruction was evidently dwelling on his mind, and from the further fact that the details of the miracle apply with remarkable aptness to the principal features of Jewish history.

How often at this time did Jesus show that the impending doom of his people was prominently in his view. Only the day before, he had wept over Jerusalem, beholding with prophetic eye her desolations, "because she knew not the time of her visitation." And the day after, he warned the rulers that "the kingdom of God should be taken from them and given to a nation *bringing forth the fruits thereof*,"* and portrayed to his disciples at length the downfall of the Jewish State. And the details of the parable are apt for this symbolic teaching. The Jewish people gave abundant signs of religious life. They were blessed with all manner of religious privileges, and they made all manner of religious professions. Those who beheld them from afar expected to find among them the fruits of religious living, upon a near approach and acquaintance. Yet their religion was all show and boast—like the produce of the fruitless fig-tree. They were without profit toward God, and cumbered the ground.

The symbolic character of the miracle is thus seen to be probable. Yet would it not be gratifying to have this confirmed? But how can we expect it to be confirmed? As intimated by the title of this chapter, we are disposed to connect the *miracle* with the *parable* of the barren fig-tree. And while, apart from any connection of the two, we may reasonably attach the symbolic meaning to the miracle just stated, it would seem that

* "If we regard the tree as a symbol of the nation, and the malediction as indicative of the nation's doom, until the end of this dispensation, the *time* of the act may be significant. Our Lord had entered Jerusalem, the day before, as her king, but he was not received in that character, except by the children. The multitudes hailed him only as the prophet of Nazareth, while the rulers plotted against his life. With that day, therefore, the day of their national visitation ended, and before he entered the city again, he portrayed in the fig-tree the nation's doom."—JONES' NOTES ON SCRIPTURE.

we are almost *compelled* to do this, if we bring the two into connection. And that the miracle was *intended* to be viewed in connection with the parable, appears in the highest degree probable, if we consider not merely the sameness of the subject—in both cases a fruitless fig-tree —but also the fact that the miracle in its symbolic character perfectly supplements and completes the parable.*

Let us glance at the parable, and then see how admirably the miracle fits it.

Jesus had been correcting the false views of his hearers, who regarded extraordinary calamities as judgments from God for particular and aggravated sins. "Suppose ye," he asks, "that these Galileans," "whose blood Pilate had mingled with their sacrifices," "were sinners above all the Galileans, because they suffered such things? I tell you, Nay; but except ye repent, ye shall all likewise perish." Again he asks, "Or those eighteen, upon whom the tower in Siloam fell, and slew them, think ye that they were sinners above all men that dwelt in Jerusalem? I tell you, Nay; but except ye repent, ye shall all likewise perish." Just before this, he had warned the people, and his enemies with them, of the crisis which was at hand, in the history of the nation. He demands of them, "Ye hypocrites, ye can discern

---

* The good Bishop HALL thus writes: "Besides that, I have learned that thou, O Saviour, wert wont not to speak only, but to work parables: and what was this other than a real parable of thine? . . . How didst thou herein mean to teach thy disciples how much thou hatest an unfruitful profession, and what judgments thou mean'st to bring upon that barren generation? Once before hadst thou compared the Jewish nation to a fig-tree in the midst of thy vineyard, which, after three years' expectation and culture, yielding no fruit, was by thee, the Owner, doomed to a speedy excision; *now thou actedst what thou then saidst."*—CONTEMPLATIONS *in loco.*

the face of the sky and of the earth; but how is it that ye do not discern this time?" And he warns them of impending judgment, and of the necessity of prompt measures in order to avoid it.*

Thus, then, just preceding the parable of the barren fig-tree, Jesus pictures the Jewish people as exposed to the imminent judgments of God, the sword of Pilate ever gleaming before their eyes ready to pierce them, the crumbling tower of Siloam ever overhanging them ready to fall in crushing destruction. And judgment is stayed, to give space for repentance. It will come in all its destructive fury, unless averted by repentance. "Except ye repent, ye shall all likewise perish."†

Then follows the *parable* of the fig-tree, for three successive years disappointing the owner of the vineyard, and spared from being cut down as cumbering the ground, by the urgent intercessions of the dresser of the vineyard, yet spared only for a single year, in the hope that renewed and yet more generous culture may result in its fruitfulness. "If it bear fruit, well; and if not, then after that thou shalt cut it down."

Thus, in the parable, is the want of fruitfulness in God's service represented as calling for judgment upon the Jewish people. And the parable leaves the people with judgment suspended over them, and ready to descend upon them in case of their continued unfruitfulness.

The subsequent history shows that the people were not brought to repentance. They failed to bring forth

---

* Luke xii. 54–59.

† "Those two calamities then are adduced as slight foretastes of the doom prepared for the whole rebellious nation."—TRENCH ON THE PARABLES.

"fruits meet for repentance." Renewed and increasing privilege only stimulated their spiritual pride and self-sufficiency and shameless boastings. They were now about to consummate their unfaithfulness by the positive rejection of the Sent and Son of God, for whose sake their nation and their religion existed. Hence the tree must be destroyed. The impending judgment must descend. The intercessor must stand aside, acquiescing though sadly in the decree of doom.

And all this is set forth in the *miracle* of the fig-tree, if we may attribute to it a symbolic character.

How deeply impressive becomes the miracle thus interpreted. As if Jesus, standing by the fruitless tree, had said to his disciples, "Remember that tree of which I told you before, so long fruitless, yet spared another year. And here is that tree, vigorous with life under its new culture, but fruitless still. The time for judgment has come." "Let no fruit grow on thee henceforward for ever."

XXIV.

Christ's Denunciation against the Scribes and Pharisees at different times Compared.

Matt. xxiii.; Luke xi. 37–54.

THE Twenty-Third of Matthew is mainly occupied with a discourse of the Saviour, of unparalleled severity, directed against the leaders of the people. "As he once commenced his sermon on the Mount in Galilee with pronouncing eight beatitudes, so he closes his last public address with pronouncing eight woes on Mount Moriah, declaring thereby most distinctly that all manifestation of his Divine love and meekness had been in vain, and must now give way to stern justice."*

Were we reading Matthew without note or comment, we should probably have no other thought than that this thrillingly solemn discourse was actually delivered at the time indicated, and substantially in the form here

---

* BAUMGARTEN in NAST. "Some have labored to show that there is a contrast between the earlier and later utterances of Jesus, indicative of a change of feelings and views. This supposition is based on the fact, that whilst at his first public appearances blessings fell from his lips, at a later period he poured forth denunciations of the cities which had rejected him. . . . The only perceivable difference is, that as he drew towards the termination of his mission, the ardent love he bore to his people expressed itself more frequently and more strongly in the form of grief at their perversity, until last of all there burst forth the prophetic warning, that their contempt of inward moral redemption must inevitably result in outward ruin."—ULLMAN'S SINLESSNESS OF JESUS.

reported. Some expositors, however, tell us that Jesus now uttered only a part of what is here recorded, and that Matthew, in making his report,—according to an alleged habit of that Evangelist,—incorporated similar sayings of the Saviour spoken at other times. The discourse as here given may seem to be connected and complete, but this, they tell us, is due to the compiler rather than to the author of these sayings.

The only reason adduced for this opinion, apart from the alleged habit of Matthew just mentioned, is the fact that Luke, in the passage above cited, has given a discourse of Christ delivered on another occasion, which strongly resembles this; some of the expressions being identical. Now, in regard to Matthew's habit of grouping things similar, we believe it to be greatly exaggerated.† Further, it seems a very insufficient reason for rejecting the common view entertained of the unity and completeness of this discourse in Matthew, that our Saviour is known to have spoken some of the same things on another occasion. Why may we not think that Christ often repeated his instructions, both as to matter and form, moving as he did from place to place, and addressing different assemblies of people? And why might he not, in a long discourse directed against a certain class of persons, repeat some of the same expressions before used in another place, in addressing the same class of persons? It were sufficiently absurd to take our conceptions of Christ's discourses in this respect from those of a parish minister preaching to a stationary congregation. Indeed we know that sometimes he did repeat himself; the very same instructions being now and

* See foot-note, p. 42.

then reported by the same Evangelist, as spoken at different times and places. Luke himself, in the very instance before us, reporting very briefly the discourse which Matthew gives at length, repeats almost *verbatim* some of the expressions which he had previously given.*

But we desire, now, further and especially to show, from a comparison of this discourse in Matthew with that in Luke, that the two are very different, and that the differences are precisely such as the altered circumstances under which the Evangelists represent them to have been delivered, seem to have demanded. Thus we shall have the best of reasons for rejecting the supposition of compilation on the part of Matthew, and for taking the discourse as he reports it for a summary of the actual discourse now pronounced by the Saviour.

It appears sufficiently clear that the denunciations of our Lord against the Pharisees, as given in the eleventh of Luke, were spoken elsewhere than at Jerusalem. It is difficult to determine where he was then performing his ministry, whether in Galilee or Perea, yet there is no difficulty in determining that he was not in Jerusalem. He was not, at that time, in the stronghold of Pharisaism. And although the exact date of that discourse is uncertain, yet plainly it preceded by a considerable period the one recorded by Matthew. The opposition of the Pharisees to Jesus, had not therefore reached its highest pitch of exasperation and malignity. From the considerations both of place and time, we should expect that discourse of Jesus, however severe in itself, to show a comparative mildness. This, as we shall presently see, is the case. We would now call

* Compare Luke xx. 45, 46, and xi. 43.

attention to the fact, that according to Luke, our Saviour did not *volunteer* his denunciations at all. They were elicited by the incidents of the occasion, and the remarks of those about him. Dining at the house of a Pharisee, the host wonders that Jesus "has not first washed before dinner." This calls for the first portion of our Saviour's utterances, extending through six verses. Then a lawyer interposes, with the words, "Master, thus saying thou reproachest us also," when Jesus speaks of the sins of the lawyers, through seven verses more, ending the conversation.

The discourse in Matthew is nearly three times the length of that in Luke. It was spoken at Jerusalem, at the end of a series of most animated encounters with the Pharisees, and in the very end of Christ's public ministry. It was volunteered by the Saviour, as his solemn and final testimony against those who, in their whole influence, were perverting the people, and who, just now, were consummating their plans for the murder of their Messiah. All things considered, the place, the time, the preceding discussions—in which the Saviour, having met every demand and disposed of every ingenious question of his adversaries, shamed them into utter silence by a wise question of his own—it seems eminently natural and befitting that the Saviour should have turned upon these princes of mischievous wickedness, and, in the presence of the people, pronounced upon them just such terrific condemnation as is here recorded by Matthew.

For, let us now observe the sharper severity of his rebukes, as here administered. In the former discourse, he had said nothing of the *greedy avariciousness* of the

Pharisees. See in what language he now characterizes this sin and its consequences: "For ye devour widows' houses, and for a pretence make long prayers: therefore ye shall receive *the greater damnation.*" Before, he had said nothing of their religious *party-zeal*. Now, his language of condemnation of this sin is equally energetic with that just given: "For ye compass sea and land to make one proselyte, and when he is made, *ye make him two-fold more the child of hell than yourselves.*" While in Luke, the Scribes and Pharisees, when once denounced as "hypocrites," are compared to "graves which appear not, and the men that walk over them are not aware of them," the comparison in Matthew is that of "*whited sepulchres,* which indeed appear beautiful outward, but are within *full of dead men's bones and of all uncleanness.*" While in Luke, he once addresses the Pharisees as "fools," he here repeatedly addresses them as "*fools and blind;*" and it is worthy of note that the word for "fool" in the Greek of Luke is a mild word, signifying "mindless" or "unreasoning," while in Matthew it is that word of intense *moral reproach* which, used by us concerning a fellow-man, puts us, as our Saviour has taught us, in peril of hell-fire.* Only in Matthew occurs that vehement and ominous appeal, "*Ye serpents, ye generation of vipers, how can ye escape the damnation of hell?*" And when we remember that John the Baptist first used this exact form of address, saying, "O generation of vipers, who hath warned you to flee from the wrath to come," when he saw many of the Pharisees and Sadducees coming to his baptism, there seems a peculiar fitness in our Saviour taking it up just at this

* Matt. v. 22.

time. For this very day, when these Pharisees, demanding of Jesus by what authority he assumed to act, were referred to the baptism of John, they refused to acknowledge it as of Divine authority.* And, as the crowning instance of our Saviour's present enhanced severity of denunciation, we may observe that whilst in Luke he sometimes uses the exclamation "woe" against the Pharisees or lawyers, and once adds "hypocrites;" here in Matthew, the long discourse is mainly sustained upon the key-note, "*Woe unto you, Scribes and Pharisees, hypocrites.*" Seven times is this same phrase uttered, sounding forth like so many successive blasts from the trump of fate.

It might also be shown that this discourse, of such terrible severity, finds an appropriate conclusion in that most pathetic lamentation of the Saviour over Jerusalem, connected by Matthew with his report of this discourse. The conclusion befits the character of the Saviour, the character of the discourse, and all the circumstances of the occasion. For he is the tender, pitying Redeemer still. His wrath is the strange wrath of the lamb. And the perverse wickedness of those whom he has just denounced is hurrying onward not only themselves, but the whole people, to a dreadful doom. No wonder that, rejected of the nation, the words with which he *closes* his ministry are these; "O Jerusalem, Jerusalem, thou that killest the prophets and stonest them which are sent unto thee, how often would I have gathered thy children together, even as a hen gathereth her chickens under her wings, and ye would not! Behold your house is left unto you desolate. For I say unto you, ye shall

---
* Matt. xxi. 27.

not see me henceforth, till ye say, Blessed is he that cometh in the name of the Lord."

Our conclusion is, that just such a discourse as this which Matthew records, is in exact harmony with the circumstances in which it is represented to have been uttered; and that so far from the similar discourse in Luke furnishing any argument against the opinion that this in Matthew was delivered substantially as here presented, it affords a strong argument in precisely the contrary direction.

XXV.

The Anointing of Christ by Mary of Bethany: The Evangelists Compared.

Matt. xxvi. 6-13; Mark xiv. 3-9; John xii. 2-8.

THE time of this occurrence was subsequent to the raising of Lazarus, and shortly preceding the Saviour's final passover. The supper was given at the house of Simon the leper, evidently a familiar friend of the family of Bethany. All the members of that family were present, Lazarus sitting at the table, Martha serving the guests, and Mary engaged in anointing the Saviour.

We may first observe the identical differences of character, ascribed to the sisters of Bethany by the Evangelists Luke and John.* In Luke, Martha appears the busy, practical, talkative woman, intent on her housekeeping, "cumbered about much serving." Mary is quiet, retired, receptive;—"who sat at Jesus' feet and heard his words." In the eleventh of John, in the narrative of the raising of Lazarus, it is Martha who first hears of the coming of Jesus to the village, showing that she, more than her sister, was in contact with outward life. Hearing of his coming, she goes to meet him; in the interview with him exhibiting great self-command and great readiness in the expression of her feelings.

* Luke x. 38-42; John xi. and xii.

Mary, meanwhile, had not heard of the arrival of Jesus. She "sat still in the house," apparently absorbed in grief. And when, at the bidding of Jesus, she came forth to meet him, she could only utter a single exclamation, being dissolved in emotion and falling at his feet. And in the twelfth of John, where the sisters reappear, they exhibit precisely the same characteristic differences, Martha honoring the Master by an active attendance upon him, "serving" the table, and Mary testifying to her feelings of profound and grateful love by extraordinary acts of devotion, having once more assumed her blessed station at the feet of Jesus.

These notices of the sisters, in Luke and in John, have no connection with each other, and the differences of character in the sisters are in each case brought to view in the most casual way, thus rendering the exact agreement of description all the more striking as a proof of the minute truthfulness of the writers.

Further than this, the fact that Martha, as shown by John, still indulged the same active and practical disposition, after the rebuke given her by Jesus and the commendation bestowed on her sister, as recorded by Luke, is highly suggestive. It intimates that our Lord, on that occasion, did not intend a general disparagement of Martha's qualities of character in comparison with those of Mary, as if he would exalt the *contemplative* disposition over the *active* in Christian character; much less that he intended to imply that Martha was not a true disciple; but rather that Martha's busy and careful disposition had, on this particular occasion, become a snare to her, leading her to overvalue the mere hospitalities of the hour, while Mary, in endeavoring to obtain a permanent blessing from the Lord's visit by attending on his instructions, had more wisely chosen.

Let us now review and compare the accounts of the anointing given by three of the historians, and observe the manner in which they illustrate one another, and together present a full picture. Matthew and Mark are much alike. John, in many particulars, is unlike either.

Both Matthew and Mark mention the house as that of Simon the leper. John omits this, saying, "there," that is, at Bethany, "*they* made him a supper." Possibly the family of Bethany had a principal concern in providing the entertainment, holding it at the house of their friend, as more commodious than their own. John alone mentions the names of the family of Bethany, the others leaving us in the dark, even concerning the person who anointed the Saviour. They speak of her most indefinitely as "a woman." All the writers tell us of the rare worth of the ointment lavished by Mary upon her Lord; yet Matthew omits the designation of "three hundred pence," given by Mark and John as its approximate value. In the parable of the laborers, we find the stipulated wages for a day's work in the vineyard, to be a penny.* Supposing the parable to be in accordance with current custom, in this particular, the box of ointment is seen to have been regarded as worth a working-man's whole year of daily labor. While Matthew and Mark speak of Mary's pouring the ointment on the *head* of Jesus, as he reclined at the table, Mark mentions further her breaking the box, and John states that she "anointed the *feet* of Jesus, and wiped

---

* Matthew xx. 1-16.

his feet with her hair; and the house was filled with the odor of the ointment."

This beautiful act of devotion was strangely followed by a scene of disquiet and angry questioning, in which the modest, shrinking Mary was no doubt greatly "troubled," and which produced the prompt and authoritative interference of the Master. The variations in the narrative become more important, and still more suggestive. Matthew speaks of "his disciples" having indignation, when they witnessed the act of Mary. The ill feeling seems to have been general among the Twelve. Mark, however, writes that "there were *some* that had indignation within themselves," as though only a part of the Twelve might have been involved. But John, be it observed, mentions only *Judas*, making him the author of the complaint against Mary. "Then saith one of his disciples, Judas Iscariot, Simon's son, which should betray him." There is, of course, no contradiction here. Evidently the opposition to Mary's act *began* with Judas, and thence spread among the disciples until it became general. The question of Judas was echoed by one and another, until the whole table was agitated.

While Matthew and Mark speak of the question about the *waste* of the ointment, all the writers show that the alternative proposed by Judas and seconded by the rest, was the disposing of the ointment for the benefit of the poor. John informs us, too, and that very explicitly, that the plea of Judas for the poor was hypocritical; that the real cause of his indignation was not the thought that the poor might have been benefitted by the sale of the ointment, but the thought that he himself might have been advantaged, by the appropriation of a share of the proceeds of the sale, according to his custom. "This he said, not that he cared for the poor; but because he was a thief, and had the bag, and bare what was put therein."

Of course the other disciples could not be charged with the hypocrisy of Judas, although they joined in his complaint. There was abundant room for an honest belief, on the part of the disciples, that the act of Mary was mistaken and censurable. The question of Judas was most plausible. Even in these days, and with the keenly discriminating judgment of the Saviour here pronounced in view, Christian people are often found taking sides in favor of Judas and against Mary. The cases are by no means rare, in which the spirit of a low utilitarianism is found ruling the church, exclaiming against all costly gifts to the honor of the Saviour as so much waste; and equally prevalent is the spirit of a false humanitarianism, which makes the relief of the poor the supreme religious duty. There were some things in which the veteran Apostles of our Lord, dulled in their affections by earth-born expectations and warped in their judgments by special reasonings, could be taught and rebuked by the conduct of a simple-minded, single-hearted woman, who, in an affectionate devotion to the person of her Lord, with humble and almost passionate gratitude, threw herself at his feet and lavished upon him her choicest treasures.

The Lord speedily comes to the relief of the loving but troubled Mary, sternly remonstrating with the disciples, approving what she has done, pronouncing it "a good work," disclosing the principle upon which the lavish employment of Mary's wealth in the manner described may be justified, even in view of the needs of the poor,* and pronouncing that wonderful prophecy of honor upon Mary, that "wheresoever this gospel shall be preached in the whole world, there shall also this, that this woman hath done, be told for a memorial of her."

It is of this prophecy that we desire to say a word, before concluding this chapter. Nothing of like form is to be found in the whole range of the gospels, or indeed of the whole Bible. The Master seems to have

---

* The principle on which Jesus justifies the conduct of Mary, seems to be this; that extraordinary tokens of love and honor done to himself are permissible on extraordinary occasions. Mary, feeling her infinite indebtedness to Christ, her brother's deliverer, her own soul's Saviour, and having few opportunities to express her grateful love and her desire to honor her Lord—not knowing indeed when, if ever, she shall have another such opportunity, had done well to seize and improve this.

Every one is disposed to give honorable and costly interment to deceased friends. The *occasion* is believed to call for it. We clothe their bodies in expensive garments; we encase them in coffins of beautiful wood—lined within and silvered without. We construct for them spacious vaults, or erect over them the monumental marble. No one asks, "Why this waste?" although nothing of it can benefit the dead. Thus is it, and thus has it been, always and everywhere. Thus was it with the Jews. And this illustration our Saviour uses, to set forth the propriety of Mary's conduct. "She has come to anoint my body beforehand for the burial." "Her anointing, under the extraordinary circumstances of the case, truly honors me, and is appropriate and commendable, as would be the case if she knew that it was the last sad rite, the last pious offering made for my sepulture."

We do not think that Mary intended her anointing as *literally* a rite of sepulture, as some seem to think. (See ALFORD.) How *could* it have this character, in her estimation? Yet the words of the Saviour have an additional significance, when we associate them with his death and burial soon to occur. It is as if Jesus had said, In the light of these, you will judge of this deed of Mary more justly. You will see that Mary did well to embrace the opportunity—the only one ever to be afforded her, for expressing her grateful love, and honoring me in the extraordinary manner which you have witnessed.

been thoroughly roused to the desirableness of affixing the seal of his unmistakable approbation to the deed of Mary, so grievously misunderstood by the whole body of the Apostles, and of sending down this instance of Christian conduct, approved by him against the expressed judgment of his disciples, for the perpetual and peculiar admiration of his people in all generations.

Now is it not most remarkable that the two Evangelists who record this prediction, and who are thereby instrumental in securing its fulfillment, do not mention the name of Mary in connection with the prediction, nor in any part of their narrative here? Yet this is the case. And, from them alone, we should never have been able even to conjecture who was the person so peculiarly honored of the Lord. We should have known nothing more than that it was "a woman." And is it not further remarkable that the Evangelist John, who gives the name of Mary in connection with the anointing, and thus permits us to associate her name with the honorable prediction of Christ, does not himself record that prediction? Yet it will be seen, upon examination, that he does not make the slightest allusion to it.

Thus does John's gospel here seem particularly intended to supplement the others. Who would part with the name of Mary of Bethany from this account? Who would remove the name from any monument recording a deserved eulogy? And, in this instance, we see Matthew and Mark erecting the monument and writing the eulogy, while John comes in with the inscription of the needed name.

Her eyes are homes of silent prayer,
   Nor other thought her mind admits,
   But—he was dead, and there he sits,
And He that brought him back is there.

Then one deep love doth supersede
   All other—when her ardent gaze
   Roves from the living brother's face,
And rests upon the Life indeed.

All subtle thought, all curious fears,
   Borne down by gladness so complete;
   She bows, she bathes the Saviour's feet
With costly spikenard and with tears.

Thrice blest whose lives are faithful prayers,
   Whose loves in higher love endure;
   What souls possess themselves so pure,
Or is there blessedness like theirs?   TENNYSON.

XXVI.

The Resolution of Judas to betray his Lord, and its Immediate Occasion.

Luke xxi. 3; John xii. 2–8.

THE Jewish Council, shortly after the raising of Lazarus, had formally resolved upon the destruction of Jesus.* Again and again, during the few days preceding his last passover, they sought to lay hands on him as he taught in the temple, but failed of their desire because of the friendly multitudes who surrounded him. Finding themselves thus baffled, they turned their attention to more secret measures; "they consulted that they might take Jesus by subtilty and kill him." They thought it best, however, to postpone the matter until after the passover festival, when there would be less likelihood of popular interference. "But they said, Not on the feast-day, lest there be an uproar among the people."†

For a year Judas had been consorting with Jesus and the Apostles only for base purposes.‡ No doubt he still hoped that Jesus would sooner or later establish a worldly kingdom, in which, as one of the Apostles, he might enjoy great worldly honor and emolument. Meanwhile his avaricious greed was to some extent gratified by frequent purloinings from the company's

* John xi. 53.   † Matt. xxvi. 3–5.   ‡ See pp. 89, 90.

little purse. Yet we may conceive that Judas anticipated with eager desire the arrival of the period of his Master's worldly exaltation, and chafed with impatience at its long delay. He had observed, too, we cannot but think, the anxiety of the Jewish Rulers to get the Master into their hands, and the manner in which they had thus far been baffled. We read now of his going privately to the Rulers, and engaging with them to deliver his Master to their power.

Concerning his crime herein, we need not entertain any extreme view. We need not imagine that it was not instigated to any extent by malice, nor that it was instigated by simple malice. His motives were no doubt base and foul, even when not simply malicious; and malice mingled in the entire transaction. His *avarice* found room for exercise, as is evident from the account of his dealings with the priests. His first question to them is, "What will ye *give me*, and I will deliver him unto you?" "And they covenanted with him for thirty pieces of silver." Possibly Judas may have hoped to precipitate upon his Master the necessity of assuming his regal powers, and erecting his throne, by the miraculous overthrow of his enemies. Possibly he may not have distinctly contemplated the death of his Master as the consequence of betrayal. Or, in the event of his Master's death, perhaps he thought of that strange saying of Christ, that in his being put to death "all things that are written by the prophets concerning the Son of man shall be accomplished." Judas may have reasoned thus; "even if he *should* be killed, it is only what he seems to expect, only what he consents to, only what he says has been predicted and predetermined.

My agency in delivering him to the priests, then, can make no difference." It seems to have been some such thought that Jesus addressed, when afterward he declared, in the presence of Judas, "The Son of man indeed goeth, as it is written of him: but wo to the man by whom the Son of man is betrayed! Good were it for that man if he had never been born."*

Yet mingling with and underlying all that was avaricious and selfish in the motives of Judas, in his act of treachery, was a diabolical *malice*. Judas was now turned in heart to be an enemy of Jesus. He had come to dislike or even hate the Saviour, and could take ready part against him with those who sought his life. This the record plainly intimates. "Then," says Luke, "*entered Satan* into Judas surnamed Iscariot, being of the number of the Twelve. And he went his way and communed with the chief priests." Judas submitted himself to the power of the Wicked One, and acted in the spirit of the Prince of Hate, when he betrayed his Saviour to his foes.

The language of the record suggests the sudden coming of a critical moment in the history of Judas; "*Then* entered Satan into Judas." Perhaps the false Apostle had often before dimly thought of betraying his Master, at some indefinite future time. But now he is fully resolved *at once* to undertake it. Satan may often before have prompted Judas, but now he takes possession of him and controls him.

It is most interesting to mark not only the critical periods in the life of this most wretched man, but also the evident occasions of their occurrence. Already we have

* Mark xiv. 21, and parallels.

considered one such period and its occasion; now we may observe another. For not only does the record, as we have noticed, here suggest a crisis in the history of Judas, but a comparison of the different writers enables us to discern a most natural occasion for it. Let us see.

Luke writes, as already quoted, "*Then* entered Satan into Judas." The question is, *When?* Bringing Luke into comparison with Matthew and Mark, we find that the time is just subsequent to the supper at Bethany.* Luke omits all reference to this supper, probably because elsewhere he records a transaction similar to that which this involves.† Thus, reading the narrative of Luke by itself, we should never imagine that the entrance of Satan into Judas had any connection with the occurrences of the supper. But what occasion for this was afforded by any of those occurrences? Surely it is not difficult, in the light of what is said in the last chapter, to perceive an easy occasion.

The anointing of our Saviour by Mary, as we have seen, was the chief incident of the supper. We have observed the angry commotion aroused against Mary, at the instance of Judas. We have observed the prompt and energetic interference of Jesus, sternly rebuking his disciples and honoring Mary. A little reflection on these

---

* We follow the order of Matthew and Mark, rather than that of John. There is nothing in the records decisive of the question of order, as between the Evangelists, and it makes no difference, so far as the line of remark made in the chapter is concerned, which Evangelist we follow. ALFORD is too positive, when, on Matt. xxvi. 6, he observes, "This history of the anointing of our Lord is here inserted *out of its* chronological place. It occurred six days before the passover."

† Luke vii. 36-50.

particulars will reveal a sufficient occasion for the crisis which so soon was reached in the life of Judas.

In the first place, it is plain that Judas was prominent and earnest in this scene. John's account fully implies this. It was he who began the controversy with Mary, and his first utterance was an outburst of indignation. The earnestness of Judas might also be inferred from the fact that Mary's act was dictated by a spirit in total contrast and thorough antagonism with that of Judas. His cold, selfish heart not only could not approve, but utterly abhorred, her beautiful act of self-oblivious, self-sacrificing devotion. Moreover, he probably uttered his remonstrance against Mary with great assurance, having, as he supposed, an unanswerable argument in the obligation to relieve the poor, and receiving the countenance and concurrence of his fellow-disciples. Thus was Judas personally and publicly committed in his controversy with Mary.

The controversy, too, it ought to be observed, bore, in no very indirect way, against the Saviour, as well as against his loving disciple. The anointing was performed on his person, was intended to do him honor, and as such was permitted by him. The controversy, sifted to the bottom, will appear very much as a personal conflict between Judas and his Master.

Bearing this in mind, and then seeing how promptly, how decisively, Jesus takes the side of Mary and opposes Judas, rebuking him, tearing his specious argument in pieces, and loading with everlasting honor her whom Judas sought to cover with reproach, is it not evident that Judas must have been to the last degree humiliated and mortified? While his fellow-disciples were all put to shame, his head must have hung lowest, his spirit must have been cut deepest. And how natural, especially when the controversy had been so nearly of a personal sort, that with his feeling of intense shame should have risen the kindlings of angry resentment against Jesus! And *now*, ah, fit opportunity! Satan enters and turns the resentment into bitter malice. And though never before resolved, it is easy for him now, with unflinching, hateful purpose, to seek the enemies of his Master, that in forwarding their plans he may revenge himself.

All this seems natural; the deductions are not forced. Yet reviewing them, let us observe the circuitous way by which we have been led, and the incidental manner in which our conclusions are established.

The Evangelist John, who alone tells us that Judas was specially displeased with Mary's act, alone omits to tell us that Judas now went to the priests to betray his Master. John enables us to see how Judas *might* now have been provoked to the deed of treachery, yet he says nothing here concerning the treachery.—Matthew and Mark, both of whom speak of Judas going to the priests immediately after the supper at Bethany, do not mention Judas in their account of the supper, and give us no clue to the probable reason for his resolving on the act of betrayal just at this time.—Luke, as already seen, omitting the account of the supper, and of course all reference to the particular conduct of Judas at the supper, narrates, just as do Matthew and Mark, his going to the priests, but prefaces his account with the words, "*then* entered Satan into Judas," without explanation.

Yet the partial narratives when put together have a completeness. Luke assures us of a crisis in Judas' life.

Matthew and Mark inform us *when* it came. John tells us *how* it came.—Luke avers that "*then* Satan entered into Judas." We ask, When did this occur? and Matthew and Mark answer, In connection with the anointing at Bethany. We ask again, What occasion did the anointing give for such a crisis? and John answers, It was our Saviour's withering rebuke of Judas.

XXVII.

Christ's saying, "I am among you as he that Serveth," and His Washing the Disciples' Feet.

Luke xxii. 27; John xiii. 1–17.

ALREADY we have observed the contention among the disciples for pre-eminence at the last passover supper. This unseemly and strange conduct we have accounted for as resulting from our Saviour's teaching concerning the consummation of his ministry now at hand.*

The contention here began just as they were seating themselves at table, and probably first took the form of rival claims for positions of honor at the table. The strong desire for such positions, was, in general with our Saviour's contemporaries, a more notable matter than we, with our habits, can easily imagine. One of the special sins of the Pharisees denounced by Christ was that of "loving the uppermost rooms" or places, "at feasts."† And one of our Lord's parables was spoken, when, dining with one of the Pharisees, "he marked how they chose out the chief rooms."‡ The strife among the disciples, arising upon the occasion mentioned, and at first having respect to the honorable places at the table, no doubt before it was done included their general claims to places of dignity in the coming kingdom of the Messiah. There was probably an earnest canvass of merits,

---

* See Ch. XVI. † Matt. xxiii. 6. ‡ Luke xiv. 7.

each pressing his own claims. The contention would be the more warm, if, as we may think not impossible, they imagined that this supper was to be signalized by some advance step being taken, in connection with it, toward the inauguration of the kingdom of God.* Luke writes, "And there was also a strife among them, which of them should be the greatest."

Jesus of course does not permit the occurrence to pass unnoticed. He interposes, with words of gentle but firm remonstrance. He tells them, much as he had done once before, that while "the Kings of the Gentiles exercise lordship over them; and they that exercise authority upon them are accounted Benefactors," it shall not be so in his kingdom and amongst his disciples.† On the contrary, "he that is greatest among you, let him be as the younger; and he that is chief as he that doth serve." And, as before, he cites his own example, representing himself as a servant of others. He asks, "whether is greater, he that sitteth at meat, or he that serveth?" and adds, in words whose full significance we shall presently perceive, "but I am among you as he that serveth."

This rebuke of the Saviour perhaps seems to us, in view of all the circumstances, strangely mild. This was now the third time that the disciples had been guilty of the same misdemeanor.‡ On both previous occasions the Master had remonstrated with them. Would it not appear that their grievous fault, thus persisted in, demanded from the Saviour something more than the simple repetition of former remonstrance? Would it not have been manifestly appropriate, if the Saviour had embraced the present opportunity, so to rebuke the vain

* Luke xxii. 16, 18.   † Matt. xx. 25–28.   ‡ Ch. XVI.

aspirings of his disciples, that they would never be likely to fall again into their present error, and to impress upon their hearts a lesson of humility utterly indelible? We could not of course affirm beforehand that our Saviour *ought* to have done this, yet we can see that if he had *chosen* to do this, it would have seemed every way appropriate to the circumstances.

Well, bringing the gospel by John into proper relations with that of Luke, we find that Jesus *actually did* what we have supposed he might most suitably have done. We find that his words in Luke, "but I am among you as he that serveth," have reference not merely to his general work of humility, but to a specific service which at that moment he undertakes. We find that for a little Jesus was literally not "sitting at meat," but moving among his disciples, performing an office of all others most servant-like.

The narrative of the feet-washing given in John, as all may readily see, comes in at the beginning of the passover-meal, and hence is to be placed in juxtaposition with the narrative before us in Luke. We encounter here, indeed, a most unfortunate mistranslation in John, which often prevents the English reader from perceiving the proper connection. We read that "supper being *ended*," Jesus proceeded to wash his disciples' feet.* The proper translation is, "supper being *made* or *prepared*." It was the *beginning* of the meal, rather than the close. Not only is this in accordance with the usage of the Greek word,† but it is equally in accordance with what we know of Oriental custom. The sandals were removed and the feet washed, on entering the house and

* John xiii. 2. † See ALFORD's Greek Testament.

taking the reclining posture at table, rather than when the meal was over and the house about to be left.

Behold then the scene. No one is at hand, as they seat themselves at table, to undertake the customary grateful but menial office. In the absence of servants, some humble disciple might well have volunteered to perform, in behalf of his Master and even of his fellow-disciples, what would so greatly conduce to their comfort. But no. The thoughts of the disciples are running in precisely the opposite direction. Not dreaming of the claims or dignity of *useful service*, they are just now at the height of their noisy strife for *superior place*. And Jesus, having rebuked them with such language as we have read, proceeds to impress upon them, by a most memorable act, his lesson of humility.

Rising from the place he had just taken,* he sets about the performance of that lowly service for his disciples, which none of them had been considerate enough to undertake even for himself. He moves silently and with great deliberation, deferring any explanation of his conduct until he is done. He lays aside his upper garments, takes a towel, binds it about him, pours water into a basin, and comes to his disciples.

No doubt the noisy debate has ceased. No doubt the whole company of the Twelve are looking on in curious wonder. Perhaps as they begin to understand what he is doing, their cheeks crimson with shame. No marvel that when the Master approaches Peter, that outspoken disciple exclaims against the proceeding. Jesus persisting in the service, and completing it, with the same deliberation which marked him at the outset, resumes his place

* THOLUCK vs. OLSHAUSEN.

at the table, and proceeds to an explanation of his conduct, the terms of which clearly show that it was the intention of the Saviour, in what he had done, to rebuke the unseemly strife of his disciples. "He said unto them, Know ye what I have done to you? Ye call me Master and Lord; and ye say well; for so I am. If I then, your Lord and Master, have washed your feet; ye also ought to wash one another's feet. For I have given you an example, that ye should do as I have done to you. Verily, verily I say unto you, The servant is not greater than his Lord; neither he that is sent greater than he that sent him. If ye know these things, happy are ye if ye do them."

Thus does the narrative in John incidentally explain and enforce the narrative in Luke, while, at the same time, as the readers of John's gospel may readily see, it directly serves the *special* purpose of that Evangelist; his gospel having a completeness of its own, while often supplementing the others. And thus do the narratives combined present a fuller picture of a most interesting scene in the Saviour's ministry than is afforded by either of them separately.

XXVIII.

Position of Judas at the Passover Table.

Matt. xxvi. 21–25; Mark xiv. 18–21; Luke xxii. 21–23; John xiii. 21–31.

THE designation by Jesus of the betrayer at the passover table, is recorded with a variety of details by the several Evangelists. In a hurried reading of the different writers, one at one time and another at another, these details not unfrequently produce confusion, instead of serving to bring the whole scene to view with graphic clearness. If, however, we will take the trouble to bring the accounts together in parallel columns, as is done in some of the Harmonies, and will then carefully compare the details and arrange them in the probable order of actual occurrence, we shall be surprised at the clearness and completeness of the representation, and also at some of the necessary inferential results.* Let us now exam-

---

* ALFORD, who along with great scholarly learning exhibits an antipathy to the Harmonists well nigh puerile, and pushes the idea of the independence of the several Evangelists to an extreme well nigh absurd, thus writes on Matt. xxvi. 20–25. "Not that I have any desire to reduce the four accounts to a harmonized narrative, for that I believe to be impossible, and the attempt wholly unprofitable." It seems much the fashion just now to decry all harmonistic study. For this reason we are the more glad to find, in the pages of the learned and pious ELLICOTT, the following: "It is much to be feared that the tendency of our more modern study of the Gospels is to regard every attempt to harmonize the sacred narrative with indifference, if not sometimes even with suspicion. . . . We may with justice most strongly urge the extreme importance, not only in a mere

ine these details, as they would thus present themselves, and observe the results.

Jesus had already exhibited much feeling, in anticipation of the treachery of Judas.* *Now*, in deep anguish of heart, he makes solemn announcement of the fact that he shall be betrayed by one of his own disciples; "He was troubled in spirit and *testified*." (John.)

See the different forms of this announcement, as reported. They were yet at table. "As they did eat," says Matthew. "As they sat and did eat," says Mark. Both Matthew and Mark precede the announcement with the emphatic, "Verily I say unto you." John, according to his custom, uses the double Verily. Luke simply says, "Behold."—Matthew and John write, "One of you shall betray me." Mark has it, "One of you which eateth with me shall betray me." Luke varies the expression more widely, "The hand of him that betrayeth me is with me on the table."

This announcement fell like a thunderbolt upon the little company of the Twelve. They saw a dreadful meaning in Jesus' words, which they had failed to see, when, in a more indefinite way and mingled with other matters, he had predicted his betrayal.† Instantly all was the anguish of grief and self-distrust and perplexity. "They began to be sorrowful." (Mark.) "They were *exceeding* sorrowful." (Matthew.) Unsuspicious of any

---

critical, but even in a devotional point of view, of obtaining as complete and connected a view of our Lord's life and ministry as can possibly be obtained from our existing inspired records. And this, let it be remembered, can only be done by that patient and thoughtful comparison of Scripture with Scripture which now finds such little favor with so many theologians of our present day.—LIFE OF CHRIST.—Foot-note, p. 216.

* John xiii. 18–20. † Matt. xx. 18, and parallels.

one of their number in particular, they "looked on one another, doubting of whom he spake;" (John;) "they began to inquire among themselves which of them it was that should do this thing." (Luke.) And each being suspicious of himself rather than of any of his fellows, "they began every one to say unto him," (Matthew,) "one by one," (Mark,) "Lord, is it I?" (Matthew and Mark.) The confusion of the disciples and the distress of the Master mingle in a general excitement.

In answer to the question, who the guilty one may be, Jesus at first responds only in general terms, that it is one of the Twelve that dippeth with him in the dish. (Matthew and Mark.) This seems to be only an emphatic repetition of what he had already declared; as if he had said, "It is indeed one of you, my professed disciples and familiar friends." To John, however, who reclined on the bosom of Jesus, and to whom Peter had beckoned that he should ask the Lord *privately*— the only apparent object of such a signal—Jesus answers, no doubt in a voice too low for the others to hear —he communicating the answer as quietly as John had conveyed the question—"He it is to whom I shall give a sop, when I have dipped it." Perhaps while Peter was signalling John, the Saviour makes that declaration, recorded by Matthew, Mark, and John, of the terrible guilt of the betrayer, even though his act instead of hindering actually accomplishes the Divine purpose,* "The Son of man goeth as it is written of him; but woe unto that man by whom the Son of man is betrayed." To this he adds, according to Matthew and Mark, those

* See p. 155.

portentous words, "It had been good for that man if he had not been born."

Judas having somewhat delayed the question which the others just now were proposing, and hoping perhaps to divert suspicion from himself, now hypocritically asks, "Master, is it I?" To this Jesus gives the emphatic response, "Thou hast said"—it is indeed you. (Matthew.) At the same time, Jesus dips a piece of bread in the dish and passes it to the traitor. (John.)

And speedily, as John intimates, Satan, who before had been busy with Judas, takes renewed and fuller possession of him; "And after the sop Satan entered into him." The knowledge that he is discovered of the Master, fires his guilty purpose. Jesus perceiving this says to him, in a voice which all hear, "That thou doest, do quickly," and he hastens forth to his damning work under the congenial cover of the darkness of night. (John.)

Such is the full and graphic representation afforded by a collation of the various incidents and expressions of the different writers. Yet, for us now, a still greater interest may be derived from these narratives, by cross-examination and the reconciliation of apparent disagreements.

We commonly imagine, from the reading of these accounts, that Jesus had plainly designated Judas as the betrayer, to the whole company, before Judas withdrew. Jesus had told John that the traitor was he to whom he should give the morsel when he had dipped it, and dipping it he gave it to Judas. So, also, Jesus had responded to the question of Judas, "Master, is it I?" in the most emphatic manner, assuring him that he was the betrayer. Must not the whole company hereby have been informed of the guilty one?

Yet, from what the Evangelist John tells us, it appears that when Judas withdrew from the company, he was still unsuspected by his fellow-disciples. Jesus gave him the ominous command, "That thou doest, do quickly," yet it is said that "no man at the table knew for what intent he spake this unto him." The disciples did not imagine that it referred to any wicked conduct. Rather, they still regarded Judas as their honored purse-bearer, and supposed that the Master looked to him as such, for the performance of useful duties connected with that position. "For some of them thought, because Judas had the bag, that Jesus had said unto him, Buy those things that we have need of against the feast; or that he should give something to the poor." It was not possible, in the nature of the case, that they should thus have regarded Judas, had they just before seen him pointed out by the Lord as the betrayer, and had they known that the terrible woe of the Master was denounced against him. Probably they came speedily to understand that he was the betrayer, when Jesus, relieved of his presence, began at once to pour forth his soul, now no longer troubled but calmed and elevated, in such words as these, "Now is the Son of man glorified, and God is glorified in him."*

How, then, shall we construe the explicit announcements made by the Saviour, first to John, next to Judas? Undoubtedly John understood from the Saviour that Judas was the betrayer. But, as already intimated, the announcement to John was probably made in a low

* John xiii. 31.

voice, which none others heard, this being easily done because of John's position, next to Jesus. And John may not have communicated his information to any one —even to Peter, the very manner of Jesus in imparting it perhaps operating to restrain him. And so, when John says, "No man at the table knew," he means no one of the disciples except himself.

But what shall we say of Christ's response to Judas? Judas asked, "Master, is it I?" and Jesus answered, "Thou hast said." Must not the whole company have thus been unmistakably assured that Judas was the traitor, and have recoiled from him in horror? Yet, as we have seen, even after this they did not suspect him, but regarded him with favor, and supposed him to be still in the confidence of his Master. How shall we solve this difficulty? The solution is not easy, save upon one hypothesis, and upon that it is extremely easy. We may at first be startled by it; we shall certainly find it suggestive. As Jesus could speak to John, without the rest of the Twelve hearing what was said, for the reason that John was next him, reclining on his bosom; so Jesus could speak to Judas, in the emphatic words, "thou hast said," without the rest of the Twelve hearing the language, if only we may suppose that *Judas was next the Saviour on the other side, or that Jesus was reclining on the bosom of Judas!*

While there is nothing in the narrative inconsistent with this supposition, there are some things which incidentally confirm it. For example, Jesus could not well have given to Judas the morsel which he had dipped, unless Judas had been near him. Besides, it would probably have excited suspicion to send the morsel to one at a distance, while to offer it to the one next at hand was to follow a customary token of friendship.

And, although it may seem a fanciful refinement, we confess that we have not been able to avoid the impression, that probably the strife for places of honor at the beginning of this supper had been led by Judas, he not being able to reconcile himself to the preference which Christ exhibited for the disciple whom he loved, without claiming for himself the position of next or equal honor on the other side of the Master.

Admitting the supposition, do we not find it amazingly suggestive? Jesus on the bosom of Judas, at the moment his black-hearted treachery was ripening for execution! And how doubly impressive becomes the Scripture spoken beforehand as prophecy, and here cited by the Saviour and applied to the betrayer, when we think of Judas as *thus* the familiar friend of Jesus, and *thus* receiving from his hand the bread of friendship, "He that eateth bread with me, hath lifted up his heel against me!"

XXIX.

The Agony in the Garden; as illustrated by the Temptation in the Wilderness.

Matt. xxvi. 36–46; iv. 1–11, and parallels.

SPECULATION may well hesitate, lest with unhallowed footstep it venture within the sacred enclosure of Gethsemane. Still it is permitted us, with subdued and reverent spirit, even to enter the garden's innermost retreat, and to ponder the spectacle of the solitary midnight wrestlings of the Son of God, amidst the deep olive-shadows, when, for the time, a more than mortal anguish had fallen upon him.*

The Master and the disciples having reached the garden, he withdraws from the company, going to the place of prayer. He is not wholly unattended. The "three chosen of the Twelve" are again with him. And now the wonderful serenity of spirit which he had before preserved forsakes him. Matthew writes that "he began to be sorrowful and very heavy." Mark's language is yet more striking; "He began to be *sore amazed*, and to be very

---

* Nothing in the pages of M. Renan is more shocking than his speculations on this most sacred scene. Elsewhere, in frequent instances, he succeeds in shrouding the dead body of his Unbelief in the draperies of an attractive Sentimentalism. Here his art was defied. He has doubtless done his best, but the veil is thin and ragged, and the corpse stares at us in ghastly hideousness.

heavy."* Not only did he experience a distressful sinking of soul, but a sudden terror seized him. The anguish was well nigh insupportable; life itself was ready to give way. He exclaims, "My soul is exceeding sorrowful, even unto death." Relief must be had, and he flies to God in prayer. He bids his disciple-companions wait and watch with him. Then going "a little further," (Matthew,) or "forward a little," (Mark,) until "he was withdrawn from them about a stone's cast," he "kneeled down and prayed." (Luke.) His very posture soon became indicative of the intensity of his feelings; for he prostrated himself on the ground, (Mark,) on his face, (Matthew,) and so—in the language of the writer to the Hebrews—"offered up his prayers and supplications with strong crying and tears unto him that was able to save him from death."

Mark first records the substance of his prayer. He "prayed that, if it were possible, the hour might pass from him." Then he indicates more exactly, as do the others, the language of Jesus. Matthew gives the words of address, "O my Father," while Mark inserts the additional word of tenderness and trust, "*Abba* Father." He prays that "the cup," that is, doubtless, the dreadful sufferings appointed to him for the coming day, may be removed from his lips.† He offers this prayer in reve-

---

* ALEXANDER *in loco* thus writes, "*Sore amazed*, a very strong Greek word denoting both surprise and consternation, and here used in its strongest sense to signify the preternatural depression and alarm, of which our Saviour condescended to partake, as the representative and surety of his people. The other verb, although of doubtful derivation, is employed by Xenophon and Plato to denote extreme anxiety and anguish."

† John xviii. 11.

rent submission to his Father's will: "if it be possible" —not otherwise.

The agony must have been protracted; for the disciples during its continuance were overcome with sleep. It was now, apparently, that, as Luke informs us, "an angel appeared unto him from heaven, strengthening him." And probably it was also in this first season of protracted supplication, that, according to Luke, his agony rose to such height and fierceness, that, even in the cold midnight air, his body, in sympathy with his rent and crushed spirit, yielded from its thousand pores great drops of clammy sweat, as of blood, rolling to the ground.

Coming to the three disciples, whom he finds asleep through sorrow, he gently chides them, administers needed warning and caution, then goes and prays the second time. Mark says, he "spake the same words." Probably this statement was not meant to be literally taken. The substance of the prayer was doubtless the same, yet from what Matthew records as the tenor of it, it would appear that now the desire of relief from his anticipated sufferings was less prominent than before. The will of his Father that he should suffer seems to have been uppermost in his thoughts, with the accompanying feeling of resignation. The language now is, "O my Father, if this cup may not pass away from me except I drink it, thy will be done."

This second season of prayer could not have been brief; for again the disciples, even incited to wakefulness as they had been by the remonstrance of the Master, were found asleep. We may infer the painfully absorbing character of the scenes through which these disciples for hours had been passing, when we see that now, with so many and such pressing inducements to vigilance, they should, to their own utter confusion, thus repeatedly be overcome with sleep.

But the conflict was not yet over. We *infer* a third season of prayer from Mark, who speaks of his coming the third time to his disciples, while Matthew distinctly informs us that "he went away again and prayed the third time, saying the same words." Perhaps the feature of acquiescence in the Divine will was, in this last exercise, yet more prominent and became all absorbing. "He was heard, in that he feared," yielding himself with holy and unhesitating submission to the Divine disposal. He received the answer to his prayer, in Divine assurances and comfort and strength, enabling him with renewed serenity of spirit to move forward through all the dreadful way of a sacrificial death appointed him.

We come now to the special subject of this chapter. It is a question of much interest,—What was the exciting cause of these dire agonies of Jesus? Not often, probably, is the experience of our Saviour in Gethsemane regarded as specifically a temptation of the devil. Yet there are strong reasons for so regarding it. The Wicked One, it is true, is not personally introduced into the narrative. Perhaps that was for the reason that the intimations of his presence given, were deemed sufficient, without an express mention of the fact.

When the temptation in the wilderness had ended, the devil departed from Jesus, as we read, "for a season." Here is an intimation that he would return again, in like manner and for like purpose with his present appearing. But when did he thus personally return to the Saviour? We are not informed of his doing so at any time. Yet we find our Saviour saying to his disciples, on the very evening of the agony in the garden, perhaps only an hour before the conflict began, when they were about leaving the Passover table to retire from the city, "The Prince of this world cometh and hath nothing in me."* Here is a distinct intimation that the devil was even now at hand, and for the purpose of a sifting temptation; and the designation of him as "the Prince of this world," looking back to him as he had last appeared in the temptation in the wilderness, when he tendered the Saviour "all the kingdoms of this world and the glory of them," seems to anticipate from him such another fierce onset as he had then made in person, and a temptation substantially of the same character with that which he then urged.

With the idea of a temptation of the devil best comports the sudden seizure of the mind of Jesus with the dread of those sufferings which he had long anticipated with composure, and which this night he had regarded from a point of such elevation that they seemed already passed.† Also we can thus all the more readily think of this whole scene, according to the account of it as "an agony." The antagonism of the Human with the Divine will of the Saviour, in a conflict such as is here described, is by no means of such easy conception, as the antagonism of Christ with the devil.

Regarding, on such grounds, the agony in the garden as a conflict of our Saviour with the Arch-adversary, we are not surprised to find many coincidences between this scene and that in the wilderness, which otherwise might

* John xiv. 30. † John xvii. 4, 5.

be deemed well nigh unaccountable. In both cases, our Saviour was in retirement; and *there,* no doubt, as *here,* for the purpose of prayer. *There,* the Tempter made three attacks; *here* Jesus prayed three times, as though his distress was as often renewed. *There* as *here,* angels appear, giving personal ministrations to the Saviour, which they do at no other time. On *both* occasions, the time is critical in the ministry of Christ. *Then,* he was about opening his public ministry; *now,* he was about closing and crowning it.

Not only so, but regarding the occurrences in the garden as a scene of temptation corresponding to that in the wilderness, there is opened to us a wider analogy. We have already seen that as the Baptism of Christ stood at the entrance of his ministry considered as a whole, so his Transfiguration stood at the entrance of what may be called his passive ministry.* Regarding the agony in the garden as a conflict with the Devil, it is seen to occupy the same relation to Christ's ministry of special suffering, which the temptation in the wilderness occupied to Christ's ministry as a whole. It was the Saviour's next most striking experience after that of the Transfiguration, and was directly introductory to his ministry of special suffering; just as the temptation in the wilderness was his next most striking experience after that of the Baptism, and was directly introductory to his whole public ministry.

In the one case as in the other, the Saviour was tempted to forego his career of humiliation. In the wilderness, the temptation addressed chiefly the side of our nature representing *Desire;* in the garden, the

* See Ch. II.

temptation addressed chiefly the side of our nature representing *Fear*. Thus, in these two grand instances of personal antagonism with the Devil, our Saviour is seen to have been "tempted in all points like as we are, yet without sin."

XXX.

The two cries of the People, "Hosanna to the Son of David," and "Away with Him—Crucify Him."

Matt. xxi. 9; Luke xxiii. 21, and their parallels.

THE most impressive instance of popular caprice found in all history, is commonly imagined to be that afforded by the two cries above recorded. One day, it is said, the multitudes were rending the skies with their Hosannas to Jesus; a few days after, they were clamoring for his blood. Popular favor is indeed most fickle, and it is not certain that those who so eagerly applauded the Saviour when his cause was in the ascendant, acted the part of faithful friends when suddenly he was found in the hands of his enemies, and his cause seemed about to be overthrown.

Yet that those who on the former occasion acted the part of professed friends, speedily turned against Jesus, and, a few days after, with one consent, being "instant with loud voices," denied him before Pilate, demanded the release of Barabbas, and "required that he might be crucified," there is no good reason for believing. Indeed the evidences to the contrary are many and convincing. The careful study of the records here, and of other Scriptures bearing upon these, will show that the crowd which clamored for the crucifixion of Jesus was substantially a different company from that which gave him triumphal entrance into Jerusalem.

Let us remember, first of all, that when Jesus made his entry into Jerusalem, the passover was at hand, and that vast multitudes were gathering to the city for the festival. Let us further remember that the ministry of Jesus had been performed mainly away from Jerusalem and its vicinity, and principally in and around Galilee. Let us still further remember that Jesus was popular in the regions where he had chiefly labored, having been followed by immense crowds, who were astonished at his doctrine, and who witnessed or even participated in his many and beneficent miracles. The chief drawback to his popularity in these regions arose from the interference of Scribes and Pharisees, many of whom were sent down from Jerusalem for the very purpose of resisting him. And let us also remember that, as the last circumstance mentioned intimates, Jerusalem was the headquarters of that Pharisaism which opposed the Saviour with bitter determination, and that the *common people* of Jerusalem, as greatly under the influence of the ecclesiastical leaders of the nation residing among them, were likewise as a body unfriendly to Jesus.* Thus in Jerusalem, during the great festivals, would be found two large sections of people, having essentially opposite relations to Jesus; first, the permanent inhabitants of the city—his enemies; secondly, those who had come up to

---

* It was not easy for the authorities at Jerusalem, always to keep the people of the city united in opposition to Jesus. An instructive instance of the favorable impression made upon the Jerusalem people by our Saviour, and of the consequent alarm and indignation of the Rulers, may be found in John vii. 25–52.

Jerusalem from Galilee and the countries adjacent—his friends.

Let us now turn to the history, and learn *first*, who they were that cried their Hosannas to the Saviour. It appears that the multitude attending on him when he entered the city, was composed in part of those who had journeyed with him just previously, and in part of those who before had reached the city. Most of those who journeyed with the Saviour belonged evidently to those districts of country in which he had chiefly labored. They had come from Galilee through Perea, joining themselves to him in great numbers, as his admiring followers.* Some of them, indeed, murmured at his consorting with Zaccheus.† Many of them, no doubt, were mistaken friends. Yet the company, as such, believed in him as a great prophet, or as the Messiah, and now that "he was nigh to Jerusalem," thought that "the kingdom of God should immediately appear."‡ Those, too, who went out from the city to meet him, were strangers in Jerusalem. The Evangelist John thus writes, "On the next day *much people that were come to the feast*, when they heard that Jesus was coming to Jerusalem, took branches of palm-trees, and went forth to meet him, and cried Hosanna."

Thus the multitude which so enthusiastically escorted the Saviour into Jerusalem, one part going before him and the other part following him,§ was made up, in both its parts, of those visiting the city. And these were to such an extent his acquaintances and friends, as to make it improbable that their rejoicing at his entrance into the

* Matt. xx. 29–34, and parallels. † Luke xix. 7.
‡ Luke xix. 11. § Mark xi. 9.

city was a sudden effervescence of feeling, produced by an unreasoning impulse which had quickly become contagious, and which once over left them to be swayed by any new and chance impulse, however diverse from the former.

We may *next* appeal to the history to learn who they were that madly vociferated the cry, "Away with him, Crucify him." An examination of this point will satisfactorily show that they were not the strangers at the feast, but were the people of Jerusalem, as distinguished from these. They were those whom the hostile Pharisees habitually controlled.

Commencing with the scene before Pilate, where this murderous cry was raised, and going back in the narrative to learn how the body of people there mentioned was formed, we ascertain that its nucleus was the company which the night before had gone forth with Judas to apprehend the Saviour. These are called in the history "a great multitude." They went in company with a military force, a "band of men and officers," being themselves irregularly armed with "swords and staves." And it is distinctly stated, that they "came from the chief-priests, and the scribes, and the elders." They were the minions of the hostile chiefs of the nation.*

The arrest of our Saviour must have occurred near midnight. He was first taken before the High Priest. "As soon as it was day," the Sanhedrim met, and Jesus being brought into its presence, judgment was soon given against him. Little time was lost in taking him before Pilate, for still "it was early." Evidently "the whole multitude of them,"† headed by the Council,

* Mark xiv. 43. John xviii. 2, 3. † Luke xxiii. 1.

could not have been very different in its composition from the multitude which went out for the arrest of Jesus. The numerous friends of Jesus, strangers in Jerusalem, lodging wherever they could, many of them doubtless spending the night outside the city, probably had not yet, in any considerable number, even heard of what was going on.

Some time, perhaps an hour or two, was spent in the first examination by Pilate, and in taking the Saviour to Herod and returning again. The crowd may have received an accession during this time, but it remained essentially the same, since Pilate recognizes it as unchanged. "And Pilate, when he had called together the chief-priests, and the rulers, and *the people*, said unto them, Ye have brought this man unto me, as one that perverteth the people: and behold I, having examined him before you, have found no fault in this man, touching those things whereof ye accuse him; no, nor yet Herod; for I sent you unto him; and lo, nothing worthy of death is done unto him: I will therefore chastise him and release him."*

And now it is that Pilate gives the people the choice between Jesus and Barabbas. And they, persuaded by the priests, demand Barabbas, and, in a general and persistent outcry, in which the priests largely share, pronounce their verdict upon Jesus in the words, "Crucify him, Crucify him."

Assuredly the history thus makes it very plain that those who clamored for the blood of Jesus, and were not afraid to utter the dreadful imprecation, "His blood be on us and our children," were not the multitude of

* Luke xxiii. 13–16.

Galileans and others who had come to the feast, and who a few days before had given him joyful entrance into the city, but rather, were the rabble of Jerusalem, long since inflamed by their leaders with hatred to Jesus, and ready, in desperate hardness of heart, under the example and influence of those leaders, to run all lengths of wickedness.

Were there any further evidence needed for corroborating our conclusion, we might find it in the addresses of Peter, made in Jerusalem on the day of Pentecost and soon after. "Peter, standing up with the eleven, lifted up his voice and said, Ye men *of Judea*, and all ye *that dwell at Jerusalem*. . . . Him being delivered by the determinate counsel and foreknowledge of God, *ye* have taken and by wicked hands have crucified and slain." "Whom ye delivered up, and denied him *in the presence of Pilate*, when he was determined to let him go . . . and desired a murderer to be granted unto you." "And now, brethren, I wot that through ignorance ye did it, as did also your rulers."*

Perhaps it may have seemed unnecessary to undertake in so serious a way the correction of a popular misapprehension; yet if the undertaking has led us to a more just view of the statements of the Sacred Records, it may be esteemed as well worthy our pains.

* Acts ii and iii. See also Acts xiii. 27.

XXXI.

Judas Repenting at the sight of Jesus Condemned.

Matt. xxvii. 3–5.

WERE the gospel history a fiction, as some have been reckless enough to assert, it would need to be regarded as a miracle of art. Such a character as that of Judas, introduced as he is, acting the part he does, and departing from the scene in the manner described, exceeds, as we think, in its terrible truth, its truth to nature depraved and acted on by higher powers of wickedness, anything known in the creations of art.

Such a character, too, is wholly *unique* in the history. In the whole Bible are found very few instances of suicide, and the gospel records are a total stranger to this crime, except in the single case of Judas. Yet the delineation is perfect.

The fact that Judas repented of his treachery, the occasion of his so doing, and the remorse with which he was filled, driving him to despair and self-destruction, afford a study of fearful interest.

Judas had been successful in his effort to deliver up his Master. At midnight he had led an armed band to the side of Olivet, where he knew that Jesus might be found, and coming upon the company of his old associates, had advanced to his Master, and according to preconcert betrayed him with a kiss.

The deed was consummated, and for a little Judas is lost sight of. Jesus is carried before Annas and before Caiaphas, and after some hours is brought to trial by the Council. We read of the other disciples, how they forsook Jesus and fled, how John and Peter rallied and followed their Master into the High-Priest's house, how *there* Peter's small courage again wholly forsook him and thrice he shamefully denied his Lord; but during this time we read nothing of Judas. Where he was, or what he was doing, we can only imagine. Yet we know that in the hours which elapsed from near midnight till the early morning, a great change came over him.

It was "yet early," when Jesus was led from the Council to Pilate's hall of judgment, and this seems to have been the time when Judas, as the record states, "repented himself" of what he had done. It was "*when he saw that Jesus was condemned.*" This language, too, makes it easy for us to imagine that Judas was a witness of his Master's trial before the Council. He heard the dreadful words of the unanimous verdict, "He is guilty of death," and witnessed the mockeries and insults heaped upon the condemned but unoffending One. He beheld the Master in the power of his enemies. He saw unmistakably the consequences of his treachery. And that sight, flashing through all the specious reasonings with which he had deluded himself, brought home to him, all hardened before, the full sense of his damning guilt. He saw Jesus condemned to death, and in an instant the horrid crime of his Lord's foul murder was charged upon his astonished soul.

And as Peter had gone out to weep bitterly for his denials of Jesus, so we may think Judas went out from the Council and the presence of his Master, not indeed under the movings of contrition, but under the bitings of remorse and the tauntings of the Devil who was not done with his victim. And can we not imagine him, pallid and frightened, roaming wildly the streets of Jerusalem, saying to himself, "What have I done? What have I done?" And as he goes, surely the money in his purse finds a tongue, and instead of soothing him with the sound of its silvery sweetness, cries with accents piercing his heart like barbed and poisoned arrows, " It is the price of blood—the price of blood."

Imagination aside, we know what was his frantic thought, under the lacerations of conscience. He will revoke his bargain with the priests, and undo his act of treachery. He will return the money and get back the Master. And we see him hastening to the temple, where he may find a portion of his employers, and coming into their presence, and holding forth the money, and exclaiming piteously and imploringly, " I have sinned in that I have betrayed the innocent blood."

Ah! what stinging power did this reflection give to the guilt of Judas—" the innocent blood!" Could he in that dreadful hour have only recalled some wrong done him by the Master, upon which to found a just resentment, or could he have thought of any conduct of the Master tending to discredit his claim to be the Messiah and the Son of God; thus giving some color of right to his own act in delivering him to the priests, or to the act of the priests in condemning him; it would not have been so difficult to bear the smitings of conscience. But to have perpetrated this deed utterly unprovoked, and wholly in behalf of the wrong and the wicked, it was more than he could bear. And unwittingly he is made a chief witness for Jesus, in a voluntary and unimpeachable testimony to his spotless innocence.

"He did not deserve this at my hands, or anything like it," is the confession of Judas. "He was innocent, and I ought to have defended him. He was innocent, and I betrayed him. Here, take the money, and spare me the guilt of his death. 'I have sinned'—'I have sinned in that I have betrayed the innocent blood.'"

But Judas miscalculated, if he expected sympathy from the priests. They had no concern, but for the benefit which inured to them from his crime. Disdainful of him in his pitiful grief, and unmoved at his testimony to the innocence of Jesus; satisfied that they had obtained secure possession of the object of their hate, and might now dispose of him as they would—let him be innocent or not—these callous wretches in cold contempt thrust Judas from their presence, with the words inspired from the pit, "What is that to us?—See thou to that."

Thus they parleyed at the door of the temple. And in his distraction, Judas seems to have pressed upon the priests, until they retreated within the Sanctuary, if he did not enter it himself.* When at last they drove him

---

* There are two words in the Greek Testament, as scholars well know, which are rendered *temple* in our version. The one of these uniformly signifies, not only the building proper, made up of the Holy Place and the Most Holy, into which only the priests were permitted to enter, but the building together with its various courts of popular assembly. It is this word which is used, whenever our Saviour is spoken of as teaching in the temple, or driving the money-changers out of the temple. The other word uniformly signifies the sanctuary proper, the building into which none might enter save the priests.

Now it is the *latter* word, which is used in the Greek, where it is said that Judas "cast down the pieces of silver in the *temple.*" And, as Arch-

off, with words of cutting and fiendish scorn, he turned upon them only to fling after them into the Holy Place the money which they had refused. "And he cast down the pieces of silver in the temple and departed."

The next thing in the record is, "and went and hanged himself." And was not everything in the probable circumstances just such as to sharpen his remorse and bring him to this end?

We may think of him as he leaves the temple, returning to the streets and roaming them more wildly than ever. The money is out of his hands, but the blood is still there. And perhaps, as he goes his impetuous and unguided way, he sometimes comes upon the crowd in front of Pilate's palace, and hears the cry, "Away with him—Crucify him;" or it may be he crosses the procession which conducts Jesus from Pilate to Herod, or from Herod back again to Pilate, and catches a sight of the lowly and innocent one, beset by the rabble and arrayed in the garments of mockery.

And thus his thoughts are soon maddening him to despair. The very elements and influences doubtless seem to conspire against him. The morning sun shines but to wither and blight him with its yellow light. The air grows thick and oppressive as with a curse. Separated by his own choice from his disciple-companions, who would now shudder at the sight of him; cast off and scorned by those who once communed and covenanted with him for their own wicked ends; having sinned too

---

bishop TRENCH observes, in his "Synonyms of the New Testament," this sets forth most vividly the despair and defiance of Judas, that he presses into the very Sanctuary and there casts down before the priests the accursed price of blood.

deeply against God and his Son to be willing to ask for pardon; and the time now hastening apace when that innocent blood which he has betrayed shall be foully shed; he yields himself to the impelling devil who has possessed him and resolves upon self-destruction.

He will close his eyes to the sickening sunlight, and escape the intolerable oppression of life, and go forever from that world which has excluded him from its pity and hope, and branded him as the object of all loathing and hate.—And over the steep, rocky hill-side, beneath Jerusalem's wall, he swings himself, thence again to fall headlong, perishing miserably.

XXXII.

Joseph of Arimathea, and his Mission.

Matt. xxvii. 57-60, and parallels.

JESUS, on the way to death, suffered every conceivable indignity. Yet having expired on the cross, his body was not only preserved from destruction, or from any serious marring of its organism, but was made the object of honorable and tender ministrations. The providence of God herein was most notable.

Had the Romans been permitted *their* way with the body of Jesus, it would have remained on the cross until it went to decay, or was devoured by ravenous birds. Had the Jews been permitted *their* way, it would have received the infamous interment commonly given to detestable criminals. God's special providence interfered to prevent both these results, and to secure a very different and an exactly befitting disposition of the body. And what was this special providence?

We might have supposed that the Apostles, or other Galilean friends of Jesus, would have been anxious to secure his body for burial. Some of them we know witnessed his crucifixion. Yet these might well have despaired of being permitted to execute any desire of their own. The body belonged to Pilate; and what prospect was there that the Governor would yield to the wishes of such persons as they—obscure ones and strangers—

especially when the Jews might be expected to resist them?

But precisely at the juncture demanding interference, there appears on the scene a person never before heard of in the history, who effectually performs the needed work, and who again immediately and wholly disappears. Seemingly he was raised up and commissioned for this special service. He is a man of position and influence, is desirous of giving the body of Jesus honorable burial, and promptly undertakes the office. All four of the Evangelists were moved to record the doings of this person, and it may be of use for us to review and compare their narratives, and thence endeavor to ascertain the causes which operated with such force as to set him upon his extraordinary performance.

All the writers designate him as "Joseph of Arimathea." Probably his birth-place was in the mountains of Ephraim, although he had now become a resident of Jerusalem. From Matthew we learn that he was "rich." It is Matthew, also, who by and by informs us, that the tomb in which Joseph buried our Lord, was "his own new tomb," thus indicating, though without declaring it, the fulfillment of Isaiah's prophecy, "He made his grave with the rich in his death." Luke characterizes him as "a good man and a just," belonging thus to the better class of Jews, and, as in the case of Simeon and Anna, indulging some correct expectations of the Messiah; "who also himself waited for the kingdom of God." (Mark and Luke.) He was also "a counsellor," (Luke,) "an honorable counsellor," (Mark,) from which we should naturally infer that he was a member of the supreme judicial tribunal of the nation. This inference is made certain by the declaration of Luke, that "the same had not consented to the counsel and deed of them." He, and probably Nicodemus, and possibly some others, were absent from that packed meeting of the Sanhedrim which gave a unanimous verdict against Jesus.* Still further, he was "Jesus' disciple," (Matthew,) "but secretly, for fear of the Jews," (John,)—he yielding unworthily to the special temptation of his high position.

Thus full is the account of this man, gathered from all the writers. He seems to have been much such a person and disciple as Nicodemus, his brother Senator, and naturally, though significantly enough, these two are presently found in co-operation, probably having previously conferred respecting their proposed work.

Joseph is already on his way to the Roman Governor, prosecuting his mission, when introduced into the narrative. The time, according to Matthew and Mark, was the evening—"when the even was come." This designation of time was very indefinite then, as it is now. The evening sacrifice occurred at the ninth hour, or at three o'clock, P. M. Luke has it, that "the Sabbath drew on." It was, by our reckoning, somewhere between three and six o'clock, P. M. Both Mark and Luke mention, as John has also done, that it was "the preparation;" and Mark explains this to mean, "the day before the Sabbath." The point needing to be observed is this, that the time remaining for the burial was short. The arrival of the Sabbath must be anticipated, and for this, prompt and even hurried measures were required.

The Pharisees, like Joseph and Nicodemus, were anxious that the burial should take place before the Sabbath

* Mark xiv. 64.

commenced, (John,) and probably the visits of the two parties to Pilate occurred near the same time. Joseph, having obtained his request, returned to the cross, making purchase of fine linen and carrying it with him. Meanwhile, and as if by previous agreement with Joseph, Nicodemus had procured the desired spices; and soon the body is lifted from the cross, wound in the linen with the spices, conveyed to the new sepulchre in the garden hard by, and there secured.

This narrative shows Joseph of Arimathea acting a most honorable part. But more than this, it shows him acting a most *courageous* part. And *that*, when we are informed that previously he had been only a *secret* disciple, through *fear*. The Evangelist Mark uses this significant language concerning Joseph—that he "went in *boldly* unto Pilate and craved the body of Jesus." And assuredly his act must have required courage. Jesus himself to all appearances overcome by his enemies and his cause hopelessly lost, it was an act of highest heroism thus almost alone to stand forth for the honor of Jesus and for the upholding of his cause.

Well may we ask, How came it to pass that he who was only a secret disciple through fear, when Jesus was popular and his cause was seemingly marching to triumph, was now so courageous? The answer to this question, that "the heroism of faith is usually kindled by desperate circumstances,"[*] does not, even if correct in itself, in the least explain the fact. At best it only places it in a class of similar facts, all of which may require explanation. The Apostles of our Lord exhibited little

[*] Prof. Brown.

"heroism of faith" amidst these "desperate circumstances."

A comparison of the records puts us, as we think, upon a rational explanation of Joseph's extraordinary conduct. And it is mainly for the sake of this explanation that such comparison has here been made.

It is strongly intimated, by all the circumstances of the case as the records present them, that the reason for Joseph's conduct was just this, that he now found himself, in the peculiar providences of God, to be the only person having any concern for the honor of Christ, who was *so situated* as to be able to procure for him an honorable burial.

The Sabbath drew on; the enemies of Jesus were hurrying to bury him with the malefactors; most of the disciples were scattered abroad, like sheep without a shepherd; those who remained were destitute of influence with Pilate for procuring the body of Jesus, and, even if they should overcome all obstacles and procure the body, might not be able to find a suitable tomb. Joseph, we may presume, was acquainted with these facts. And he knew further that *he* had influence with Pilate— that *he* might be able to secure the body; and, still further, *there was his own new tomb*, hard by the cross, without an occupant, standing ready to receive the body of Jesus.

Did not all the indications of that solemn and eventful hour point to Joseph, as *the man* upon whom was devolved the work of rescuing the body from the infamy fast preparing for it, and giving it honorable sepulture? Must he not have felt that the crisis had arrived, when he must banish his fears and boldly avow his attachment to Jesus, or utterly and forever renounce all pretence of friendship? It was, as we cannot but think, under the pressure of these circumstances, so admirably adapted to test the reality of his discipleship, and "kindle his faith" for heroic achievement, that he went in boldly unto Pilate, and consummated the burial of his Master.

Supposing this explanation to be correct, the conduct of Nicodemus is just what we might have expected. Of like character with Joseph, and feeling to some extent the force of the same providential circumstances, he co-operates with Joseph. Yet it is not Nicodemus who owns the convenient tomb, and the circumstances do not so fully devolve on him the responsibilities of the occasion. Hence, it is exactly natural that while his courage is developed to a new degree and he is led to act a worthy part, he should still be seen only as the helper of Joseph, who remains the hero of the occasion.

XXXIII.

Jesus, after his Resurrection, appearing first to Mary Magdalene.

Mark xvi. 9; John xx. 11–18; Matt. xxviii. 8–10.

In no part of the Gospel History is it so difficult to reduce the accounts of the Evangelists to harmony, as in the narratives of the events immediately following the Resurrection.

Some persons—unbelievers—declare the accounts hopelessly contradictory, and charge the writers with fraud and falsehood. Others, who have implicit faith in the records, and who believe that seeming inconsistencies would be wholly relieved, had we a full knowledge of the actual occurrences, doubt whether it is possible with our present knowledge to relieve them, and therefore discourage all attempts in this direction. Others still, and among them probably the majority of wise expositors, not professing to find a complete narrative in any blended account of the four writers, hold that apparent contradictions may be removed by the supposition of certain circumstances having existed and certain events having occurred, which, although not recorded, are within the limits of easy probability. This method of reconciling seeming discrepancies is everywhere recognized as legitimate, under similar conditions, and we cannot imagine why it should be rejected here.

The fact of considerable diversity in the statements

may be rationally accounted for. Each writer had his own point of observation of the facts occurring. Each had his special end in view, in selecting and recording those which he has given. And further, it may reasonably be supposed, that any apparent confusion in the narrative is the natural result of a confusion which actually existed in the movements of the disciples. When we reflect for a moment on the fact that the disciples were strangers in Jerusalem, and probably on the night preceding the Resurrection lodged some in one place and some in another—on the fact that the first tidings from the sepulchre came early in the morning— and on the fact that these tidings were of a most astounding character; is it not evident that some confusion of movement *must* have occurred? There would be a hurrying to and fro. Some would be going to the sepulchre, while others were returning from it. The sepulchre being visited at different times, by different parties, the changes taking place would give rise to different reports concerning what was there seen. Under these circumstances, to demand that each of the writers, telling his own story from his own point of view and for his own particular purpose, should compose a narrative easily falling in with and fitting all the others, is simply preposterous. Such a demand would be reasonable, as some one has suggested, only on the supposition that the whole company of disciples marched to the tomb, by a programme previously arranged.

It is our object, in this chapter, to show how one of the most troublesome apparent disagreements in the records may be reasonably explained.

In the gospel by John we have the account of an interview of the risen Jesus with Mary Magdalene at the sepulchre. Mary is evidently alone.—In Mark's gospel, we have the distinct statement that Jesus appeared *first* to Mary Magdalene. We can hardly help the conclusion that the interview which John records is that to which Mark refers, and was Christ's first appearance to mortal vision after his Resurrection.—Yet, from Matthew's account, we obtain the impression that Jesus first revealed himself to the company of women, who, according to the first three writers, came early in the morning to the sepulchre, Mary Magdalene being then with them. And he revealed himself to them, not at the sepulchre, but after they had fled from it, going in obedience to the command of the angels to bring word to the disciples of the Resurrection. Matthew writes, "And as they went to tell his disciples, behold Jesus met them, saying, All hail. And they came and held him by the feet, and worshipped him."*

Now how are we to believe, without doing violence to the narratives, that Mary Magdalene, alone, and at the sepulchre, was the *first* to look upon the risen Saviour?

There seems to be no difficulty in the supposition, that when the company of women, including Mary Magdalene, approached the sepulchre early in the morning, and found the door open, Mary, without waiting until the angels made known the fact of the Resurrection, under the belief that the sepulchre had been rifled of its occupant, separated herself from the company and hastened

---

* We follow the received text, although some of the critics reject the phrase, "and as they went to tell his disciples." ELLICOTT is disposed to find relief from the difficulty mentioned by adopting the view of these critics. Life of Christ, p. 351. This we think unnecessary.

to bring the tidings to Peter and John. The Evangelist John writes concerning Mary, when she saw that the stone was taken from the sepulchre, "Then she runneth and cometh to Simon Peter, and to the other disciple whom Jesus loved, and saith unto them, They have taken away the Lord out of the sepulchre, and we know not where they have laid him." John indeed writes as if Mary going *alone* to the sepulchre had made this discovery, when he says, "The first day of the week cometh Mary Magdalene, early, when it was dark, unto the sepulchre, and seeth the stone taken away;" yet obviously he thus writes because it was Mary alone who gave the information to himself and Peter. He was intent, not on the visit of the women but on his own visit, and was showing how it came to be made. Mary's language, as John gives it, distinctly intimates that she had been at the sepulchre in company with others. She says, "*we* know not where they have laid him."

Thus, then, was Mary probably separated from the company of the women. The two disciples ran to the sepulchre, yet did not arrive until after the women had left, and did not meet them on the way. The disciples made their observations and departed, Mary meanwhile having followed them, and having reached the sepulchre perhaps not far from the time they left it. And now, remaining there alone, opportunity would be given for the interview with her described so affectingly by the Evangelist John.

Yet the principal question remains unanswered; the question, How can this interview be consistently conceived of as occurring *before* that with the company of women mentioned by Matthew, so as to be regarded the *first*, according to the declaration of Mark? There is a way, we think, in which this may easily be done, without violence either to the narratives or to the manifest probabilities of the case.

All difficulty is here created by the gratuitous supposition that our Saviour appeared to the women *soon after their flight from the sepulchre, and in its immediate vicinity.* We say *gratuitous* supposition. There is not the slightest evidence in its favor. So far as the record goes, we have the language, that "as they went to tell his disciples, Jesus met them." It may be admitted that the first impression produced by this language is favorable to the supposition stated. Yet nothing is plainer than the fact that these records are of a condensed and summary sort, and were not always intended to give at the first glance accurate impressions of the details of time and place. For example, Matthew says nothing of any interview of our Saviour, after his Resurrection, with any of the Apostles *in Jerusalem*, and, according to the first impression received from the reading of Matthew's account by itself, Jesus ascended to heaven *from Galilee*. And the narrative in Luke, read by itself, gives the impression that our Saviour ascended from near Jerusalem, on *the evening following his Resurrection.* We know from the Acts that he ascended from near Jerusalem, forty days after his Resurrection. We may not, then, here insist on *first* impressions. We must avail ourselves of all the information afforded, and thus secure, so far as may be, *right* impressions.

Matthew writes, as we have seen, that "as they went to tell his disciples, Jesus met them." But *where* were the disciples, and *how long* did it take the women to find them? The common supposition seems to be, that the company of the Apostles all lodged in Jerusalem, at one and the same place, and that the women knew just where to find them. The probabilities, however, are to the contrary of this. Being strangers in Jerusalem, and the city now overflowing with the multitudes who had come to the passover, probably the Apostles were much scattered; perhaps most of them were lodging with their friends at Bethany, or elsewhere amidst their familiar haunts on the Mount of Olives.* Peter and John, we may think, lodged in the city. John was to some extent acquainted there, and seems to have had there a place of temporary abode, to which he took the mother of our Lord.† And Peter and John were together, wherever it was they were staying.‡ The last we read, before this, of the rest of the eleven, they were scattered on the Mount of Olives, and not until the evening of the first day of the week do we learn of any gathering of the company in Jerusalem. Even then Thomas is absent,§ and the rest are rejoicing over the appearing of the Lord to Simon, showing that *he* had been separated from the others.‖

It seems altogether probable that the women, charged with the message to the disciples, were some length of

---

* No doubt at the festivals strangers were compelled to seek lodgings through the surrounding country, out to a considerable distance. Thus probably Simon the Cyrenian was coming in from his night-abode in " the country," to the morning sacrifice, when he was taken and compelled to bear the cross of Jesus; and thus Cleopas and his companion may have had their place of temporary residence at Emmaus, and may have been going to it for the night, when joined by Christ.

† John xviii. 16; xix. 27.   ‡ John xx. 2.   § John xx. 24.
‖ Luke xxiv. 34.

time in finding them. Perhaps they first came into the city, the sepulchre according to the old tradition being a short distance from the *western* wall, going first in quest of Peter and John whom they knew to be lodging there. And we may suppose, that not finding these disciples, who had already started for the sepulchre on the intelligence given by Mary, they passed on through the city *eastward* and out to the Mount of Olives, in search of the others.

And it may have been *in this latter part of their long walk,* " as they went to tell his disciples," that, in some of the seclusions of Olivet, the Saviour, *having already appeared to Mary at the sepulchre*, and transferring himself in his resurrection-body at will, *revealed himself to them*.

By this method of probable conjecture, we avoid the difficulty suggested, and were there nothing in the records going directly to confirm the conjectures made, we need not hesitate to accept them, so long as nothing in the records is found to contradict them. But it so happens, that a passage in the gospel by Luke, in a most incidental way falls in with these conjectures, and with our inferences from them, in a manner remarkably to confirm them. Let us see.

The two disciples going to Emmaus, who plainly were familiar friends of the Apostles,*—having started from Jerusalem not far, we may suppose, from the middle of the day, give to the unknown person who has accosted them, the following statement of the facts known to them on leaving the city. They say, " Yea, and certain women also of our company made us aston-

* Luke xxiv. 22, 23.

ished, which were early at the sepulchre. And when they found not his body, they came, saying, that they had also seen a vision of angels which said that he was alive." Evidently this was the same company of women, of whose interview with the angels the first three Evangelists tell us. Yet when they met these disciples in the city, they spoke only of the vision of angels which they had seen, and of what the angels had told them, *saying nothing of having seen the Lord*. Must we not suppose that the interview with him had not yet occurred? Not at their first flight from the sepulchre, as we again see, did the Lord reveal himself to these women. Sufficient time elapsed, as is here intimated, for him to appear, according to Mark's statement, "*first* to Mary Magdalene, out of whom he had cast seven devils."

XXXIV.

Christ's saying to Mary Magdalene, " Touch me not: for I am not yet Ascended to my Father."

John xx. 17; xvi. 16; xiv. 3.

MARY was alone at the sepulchre, Peter and John having recently withdrawn. Full of the thought that the body of her Lord had been stolen away, she stands there weeping. Presently, her tears still falling, she stoops into the sepulchre, and beholds, what Peter and John had not seen, two angels clothed in white.

It is remarkable that at this sight Mary evinces no surprise. She is sufficiently composed to observe the exact position of the angels, "sitting, the one at the head, and the other at the feet, where the body of Jesus had lain." And when they address her with the soothing remonstrance, "Woman, why weepest thou?" she answers with the utmost calmness, and from the fulness of her heart, "Because they have taken away my Lord, and I know not where they have laid him."

Behold the might of love! She did not fear; for in her heart was no room for fear. "Perfect love casteth out fear." At that moment, Mary would doubtless have little recked it, had the earth opened before her to swallow her up.

Yet, having answered the question of the angels, she rises, as with womanly dignity, to retire. As she rises, she partially turns, and in so doing catches a glimpse of some one standing back of her. Her eyes are filled with tears; perhaps the morning has not far advanced; possibly Jesus is different in appearance; above all she is not expecting to see him alive. At any rate she fails to recognize him.

He addresses to her the same question of remonstrance which the angels had asked, and still his voice is that of a stranger. She gives him a courageous reply, such as only the fulness of love would dictate. Supposing him, very naturally, to be the gardener, and thinking that probably it is he who has removed the body of her Lord, she cries, "Sir, if thou have borne him hence, tell me where thou hast laid him, and I will take him away."

But it is Jesus. And now he discloses himself to her, even through all the obstacles which before had prevented her from recognizing him. And how does he make himself known? He does it instantly and completely, by the utterance of a single word. Yet that word is her *name.* "Jesus saith unto her, *Mary.*"

No word comes so near to us as our name; none searches so closely after our personality, and carries so fully with it our very selves. And this one word, perhaps pronounced by the Saviour in his old familiar tone, was a quick and full revelation. Not a doubt remained as to who he was, and the full sense of her relations to him as his disciple came rushing upon her soul with overwhelming power. Turning completely round, she exclaims, "Rabboni," "My Master," and probably, in the transport of her feelings, is ready to cling to him, never more to be separated. Jesus, however, checks her movement, saying, "Touch me not; for I am not yet ascended to my Father."

The prohibition, "Touch me not," is regarded as one of the sayings of our Lord most difficult of interpretation. THOLUCK, after mentioning a long list of varying opinions concerning it, expressed by leading expositors, declares himself unable to adopt any one of them with confidence, and declines offering any independent judgment. We would venture to ask, whether the reason assigned for the prohibition, may not be expected to throw some light on the prohibition itself?—whether, indeed, in the ambiguities of the one, the other may not be looked to for a decisive settlement of the meaning?

Fixing our regards, then, upon the reason assigned;— "for I am not yet ascended to my Father," let us revert to our Saviour's sayings upon this point, and see if we can discern in them any reason adapted to restrain the probable action of Mary.

One of the most remarkable of these sayings is the following, "A little while, and ye shall not see me; and again a little while and ye shall see me, *because I go to the Father.*"* The disciples were at a loss to understand this saying, and inquired concerning it among themselves. And Jesus explained it, much to their satisfaction, on this wise, "I came forth from the Father, and am come into the world; again I leave the world, and go to the Father."† Before this, Jesus had declared,

---

* John xvi. 16. The critics would omit from this verse the clause, "because I go to the Father." The omission, however, makes no difference; for this verse looks directly back to the 10th verse, "because I go to the Father and ye see me no more."

† John xvi. 28.

"I go to prepare a place for you. And if I go and prepare a place for you, *I will come again and receive you unto myself; that where I am, there ye may be also.*"*

Now supposing Mary to have been familiar with such teachings of our Lord—and the fact that he spoke to her as he did implies this familiarity—is it not natural to suppose that when she first recognized the risen Saviour, her thought was that Jesus in death had left the world and gone to the Father, and that having returned to life, he had now come from the Father? How exactly would this suit his very words, "a little while and ye shall not see me, and again *a little while and ye shall see me, because I go to the Father?*" And, of course, so thinking, Mary would further think, "he has now come to take his disciples to himself, that they may abide with him for ever, even according to his promise, 'I will come again and receive you unto myself, that where I am, there ye may be also.'"

And was it not in view of such misapprehensions as these that Jesus said, "Touch me not?" As if he had said, "You are mistaken in supposing that I have now come from the Father, and I must wholly disappoint you. 'I am *not yet* ascended to my Father,' and hence cannot now take you to myself. Earthly fellowship can no longer be permitted, and the time has not come for the heavenly. Therefore cling not to me; but instead, go from me and resume the life of service; 'go to my brethren, and say unto them, I ascend unto my Father, and your Father, and to my God, and your God.'"

* John xiv. 3.

XXXV.

The Incredulity of Thomas; as Overcome in like manner with that of Nathanael.

John xx. 24–29; i. 48, 49.

Through the week following our Lord's Resurrection, the unbelieving Thomas had been saying to his fellow-disciples, "Except I shall see in his hands the print of the nails, and thrust my hand into his side, I will not believe." Let us observe how this extreme incredulity was overcome.

Faith in the Resurrection of Jesus was not for the disciples an easy matter. Their very confidence in the Messiahship of Jesus prevented them from regarding his death as possible, until he should have "restored again the kingdom to Israel." They did not interpret aright his predictions concerning his death. Perhaps they attached to them no definite meaning whatever. Their dominant and absorbing feeling led them to anticipate with confidence his triumph over all opposition, in the speedy establishment of his kingdom. When, unresisting and as if helpless, he was arrested before their eyes, bound and led away, and then shamefully put to death, they were utterly confounded. In the sudden prostration of their hopes, they could not at once think that, like as his predictions concerning his death had now received a literal fulfillment, so might they anticipate his literal Resurrection. All was dismay, and the dejection of deepest despondency.

Thus none of them credited the first reports from the tomb. Mary Magdalene "went and told them that had been with him as they mourned and wept. And they, when they had heard that he was alive, and had been seen of her, believed not." The company of women reported the same things. "And their words seemed to them as idle tales, and they believed not." Not until he had actually appeared to one of their own number, to Peter, did they credit the joyful intelligence.

On the evening following the Resurrection, Jesus appeared in the midst of the company of the Apostles, and after "upbraiding them with their unbelief and hardness of heart," showed them his hands and his feet, and ate before them, and discoursed to them. As might have been expected, they were hereby lifted from the depths of despondency to the heights of joy. "Then were the disciples glad when they saw the Lord."

From this meeting of the Lord with his Apostles, Thomas was absent. Even more incredulous than his brother disciples, he probably felt an indifference to what was going on. He treated with even greater contempt the reports concerning the Resurrection, and now that his Master was dead, hoped for nothing further.* If, on the day following the Resurrection, he had been in the city at all, perhaps, like the two disciples going to Emmaus, he had left it, amidst the eventful incidents rapidly occurring, and gone to his abode in the country.

The records do not indeed directly charge Thomas

---

* For an admirable discussion of the character of Thomas, and of his behaviour at this juncture, see Dr. Hanna's "Forty Days."

with guilty neglect, in failing to be present with his fellow-disciples, yet they strongly imply it. The gathering of a deeper cloud upon him, in whose gloom he was left to walk for many days, seems like an intended chastisement for wilful error.

Not having been present, "the other disciples therefore said unto him, We have seen the Lord." Probably they lost no time in making this joyful communication. Probably they fully rehearsed the particulars of the Master's interview. Yet so deplorably dark had become the mind of Thomas, this explicit testimony of the whole company of his fellow-Apostles made no impression upon him, except to prompt the most unreasonable exactions in order to his faith. *They* had been permitted to look upon the Lord, and had been invited to handle him, that they might know he was no ghostly apparition; and now Thomas declares that unless *he* has the same opportunity, and actually avails himself of it, to his satisfaction, he will not believe. Incredulous as were the other disciples, the testimony of Peter that he had seen the Lord was gladly credited. Thomas persisted in his unbelief against such testimony multiplied to tenfold strength. If *they* deserved the upbraidings of the Master, how much more richly Thomas.

Yet he was a true disciple, though now under strong temptation. The Saviour had not forgotten him, but doubtless had borne him tenderly in mind, and had prayed for him, that his faith might not utterly fail. And the Saviour will presently bring him to suitable feelings. The *method* of the Lord's procedure herein is highly suggestive.

He leaves the guilty disciple for a time to the unhappiness which he has wrought for himself. Indeed Thomas is not to be restored, until he has repented of his fault in absenting himself from his brother Apostles and has returned to their company. Not until a full week has elapsed, and they are assembled again much as they were before, does Jesus appear to them and to Thomas. The mode of his entrance among them is again the same, tending to create doubt concerning the reality of his being in the flesh. He does not condescend to make the way any easier for Thomas' reasoning incredulity.

This interview seems to have been granted with a special view to the restoration of the erring disciple; for no sooner does Jesus appear and bestow his salutation, than singling him out, he addresses him. And how must the words of the Master have thrilled the soul of the doubter! He hears *the precise language of his own unbelief*—that which he has been repeating to himself day by day, and with which he has obstinately met the arguments and representations of his fellow-disciples. "Then saith he to Thomas, Reach hither thy finger, and behold my hands; and reach hither thy hand, and thrust it into my side; and be not faithless, but believing."

And now we have reached the point of our special inquiries. The most frequent impression with Bible readers appears to be, that upon this offer of our Saviour, Thomas proceeded to inspect and handle the person of the Master, and thereupon came to faith. Can this impression be correct? It is scarcely possible. Our view of the procedure of our Saviour, so long as we retain this impression, is shallow and unworthy. Not after this fashion, assuredly, would the Saviour gratify and honor the unreasonable and even wicked demands of his tempted disciple.

Both the narrative itself, and the analogy of our Saviour's dealings elsewhere, suggest a different view.

Two things in the narrative strongly imply that Thomas did not accept the proposal of Jesus, but was otherwise brought to faith. The *first* is the statement which Christ afterward makes. He says, "Thomas, because thou hast *seen me*, thou hast believed." Here no further help to faith of an outward sort is recognized, than simply the visible presence of the Saviour. The *second* is the evidently *instantaneous* recognition by Thomas, at the very words of the Master, not only of the identity of Jesus and the reality of his Resurrection, but of his *absolute Divinity*. This seems utterly inconsistent with the impression so commonly entertained.*

From the teachings of the passage itself, we cannot but think that Thomas was brought to faith on this wise. Probably before this interview he had begun to see the unsuitableness of his demands, and secretly to regret that he had insisted on them. His relentings had been such as to bring him back to the company of his brethren. And now, in the presence of the Saviour, whom he finds

---

* It is with surprise that we find ELLICOTT thus writing, "We mark with adoring wonder, how the personal test which the Apostle had required, was now vouchsafed to him." And again, "With his hands on the sacred wounds, with evidence most distinct that He whom he was permitted to touch was *man*, the convinced disciple, in terms the most explicit, declares him to be *God*."

How much more satisfactory Bishop HALL—"I do not hear that when it came to the issue, Thomas employed his hands in this trial: his eyes were now sufficient assurance: the sense of his Master's omniscience, in this particular challenge of him, spared, perhaps, the labor of a further disquisition."

to have been conversant with his unbelieving thoughts, although uninformed of them from any human source; whom he finds to have been reading his heart *with omniscient eye*, and to have been sorrowfully watching over him in all his wayward and guilty course; the conviction flashes on his soul, that it is, it can be, none other than his gracious Master, not only risen from the dead, but clothed with every attribute of Divinity. And prostrating himself, he utters the cry of adoring faith, " My Lord, and my God !"

The most striking analogy to the case of Thomas, is that afforded by Nathanael. And in that instance, be it observed, it is evidently the sudden and resistless conviction of *the omniscience* of Jesus, which is followed by instant and implicit faith.

Nathanael was disposed to doubt. When Philip announces to him the happy tidings, "We have found him of whom Moses in the law and the prophets did write, Jesus of Nazareth, the son of Joseph," Nathanael is all incredulous. He responds, " Can there any good thing come out of Nazareth?" Yet going with his friend, he soon finds that Jesus has some correct idea of his character. Jesus pronounces him " an Israelite indeed, in whom is no guile," and then, at the question of Nathanael, " Whence knowest thou me?" gives Nathanael to understand that he knows *all things*, that his omniscient eye had been watching him in the secret place of wrestling prayer under the fig-tree; whereupon Nathanael exclaims, in the fulness of his unhesitating faith, " Rabbi, thou art the Son of God; thou art the king of Israel."

Jesus approves the faith of Thomas; yet as it was a

faith which needed to be helped into exercise by the personal presence and address of Jesus, he disparages it in comparison with a more ready and unquestioning faith, which would not reject the testimony of others. "Thomas, because thou hast seen me, thou hast believed; blessed are they that have not seen and yet have believed."

Our Saviour's treatment of Thomas accords with the Divine dealings with men generally, in the province of spiritual matters. Those who entertain speculative doubts concerning religion, are not commonly brought to true faith, by having their arguments of unbelief gone over in detail and refuted. These are commonly left to stand in full force. Yet they no longer have power, or are even remembered, when the Spirit of God has made known the Divine adaptations of the gospel to the deep needs of the soul. These doubts all vanish of themselves, like ghosts to their graves before the morning sun.

We close these studies in the gospels, listening to the benediction of the Master upon those who "have not seen and yet have believed," a benediction freighted with encouragement to us, who live between his first and his second appearings, and who in reference to the past and the future can humbly say, "Whom not having seen we love; in whom, though now we see him not, yet believing, we rejoice with joy unspeakable, and full of glory."

www.ingramcontent.com/pod-product-compliance
Lightning Source LLC
Chambersburg PA
CBHW020824230426
43666CB00007B/1092